The Mayor of Casterbridge for English Acquisition and Anti-Alcohol Sensitization

Augustin Orsini MENDOME MBANZOGUE
Dr. Ralph OBANDJA BOYO

Copyright © 2022 Augustin Orsini MENDOME MBANZOGUE, Dr. Ralph OBANDJA BOYO
Copyright © 2022 Generis Publishing

All rights reserved. This book or any portion thereof may not be reproduced or used in any manner whatsoever without the written permission of the publisher except for the use of brief quotations in a book review.

Title: *The Mayor of Casterbridge* **for English Acquisition and Anti-Alcohol Sensitization**

ISBN: 979-8-88676-429-1

Author: Augustin Orsini MENDOME MBANZOGUE, Dr. Ralph OBANDJA BOYO

Cover image: https://pixabay.com/

Publisher: Generis Publishing
Online orders: www.generis-publishing.com
Contact email: info@generis-publishing.com

TABLE OF CONTENS

General Introduction 9
Literature Review 13
Part One: Theoretical Framework 17
Chapter I: Clarification of Key-Terms 19
    I.1. Thomas Hardy 19
        I.1.1. Biography 19
        I.1.2. A Selected Bibliography 19
    I.2. The Mayor of Casterbridge 20
        I.2.1. Background, Context, and Category of the Book 20
        I.2.2. Characterisation 21
        I.2.3. Plot 22
        I.2.4. Setting and Time 23
    I.3. Authentic Source 23
    I.4. Language Acquisition 24
    I.5. Alcohol 25
    I.6. Sensitisation. 25

Chapter II: Some Suitable Approaches and Methods to Enable Language Acquisition and Sensitise to the Dangerousness of Alcohol Intake at Pupils' 27
    II.1. Suitable Approaches to Encourage Interaction and Self-Moral Education at Pupils' 27
        II.1.1. Language-Based Approach 27
        II.1.2. Theme-Based Approach 29
        II.1.3. Moral-Philosophical Approach 29
    II.2. Some Suitable Methods to Facilitate Language Acquisition at Pupils' 31
        II.2.1. Student-Centredness 31
        II.2.2. The Direct-Method 32

Chapter III: The Consumption of Alcohol: A Rampant Phenomenon in Gabon 35
    III.1. Synopsis: Harmful Effects of Alcohol Consumption by Pupils 35
    III.2. Some Factors Inherent to Alcohol Intake by Pupils 37
        III.2.1. Bar Activities near Schools 37
        III.2.2. Lack of Strict Adulthood Check to Enter Drinking Places 38
        III.2.3. Alcohol Advertisement Near Schools 39
    III.3. Governmental and Nongovernmental Action against Alcohol Intake at Pupils' 40

III.3.1. Government Policymaking to Protect Pupils from Alcohol Intake 41

III.3.2. Anti-Alcohol Sensitisation Campaigns in Gabonese Schools 43

III.3.3. Teachers' and Parents' Implications in Anti-alcohol Sensitisation 45

Chapter IV: Some Educational Articulations from the Novel to Raise Awareness on the Dangerousness of Alcohol Intake at Pupils' 49

IV.1. Impelled by Drunkenness, Henchard Sells His Wife 49

IV.2. The Impactful Power of Abstinence: Henchard Becomes a Teetotaller and Succeeds in Business 51

IV.3. Inebriated, Henchard Ridicules Himself in Public 52

Chapter V: Some Proposed Activities to Implement *The Mayor of Casterbridge* in English Classes 55

V.1. Role-play as an Interactive Activity to Raise Awareness on the Dangerousness of Alcohol Intake 55

V.2. Debate/Discussion on Henchard's Full Responsibility for his Wife's Sale 56

V.3. Dictation to Improve Writing and Listening Skills at Pupils' 57

Conclusion of Part One 57

Part Two: Experimentation Phase 60

Chapter VI: Data Collection and Analysis 62

VI.1. Data Collection 62

VI.1.1. Area of Study 62

VI.1.2. Target Population 62

VI.1.3. Research Strategy 62

VI.1.4. Data Collection Instruments 63

VI.2. Results and Analysis 63

VI.2.1. Results from Pupils' Questionnaire 63

VI.2.2. Results from Teachers' Questionnaire 69

VI.2.3. Assessment 73

Chapter VII: Experimental Lessons 74

VII.1. Lesson Plan 1 74

VII.2. Lesson Plan 2 79

VII.3. Strengths and Weaknesses of the Two Lessons 87

VII.3.1. Strengths of the Lessons 87

VII.3.2. Weaknesses of the Lessons 89

Chapter VIII: Difficulties Encountered and Suggestions 92

VIII.1. Difficulties Encountered 92

VIII.1.1. Inquiry Difficulties 92

VIII.1.2. Implementation Difficulties 92
VIII.2. Suggestions 93
Conclusion of Part Two 94
General Conclusion...96
REFERENCES...98
APPENDICES 104
Appendix 1. Pupils' Questionnaire. 104
Appendix 2. Teachers' Questionnaire.. 106
Appendix 3. Text: Michael Henchard Becomes a Teetotaler[1]... 107
Appendix 4. Text/Script: Drunk, Henchard sells his Wife Susan for five guineas................ 108
Appendix 5 110
Appendix 6 111

General Introduction

English is learned at school as a foreign language (E.F.L[1]) in Gabon. Its teaching process requires teachers to use authentic materials such as extracts from novels to design activities destined to improve the four communication skills (listening, speaking, reading, and writing) for an effective acquisition by pupils. These texts are commonly used for their political, economic, social or cultural contents. The main goal of such an initiative is to gradually improve pupils' general knowledge, transmit them moral values, and encourage their positive personal development. Surprisingly, these texts are generally taken from African novels.

Because the realities depicted in African novels strongly resemble Gabonese social realities, teachers are impelled to consider African literature as the most immediate and reliable source to find social and educational inputs for the personal development needs of Gabonese pupils. They unfortunately use little of American literature extracts, and even least of British ones.

Accordingly, we notice that the use of African literature texts is pre-eminent in English classes. The texts are mostly extracts from novels such as *Things Fall Apart* by Chinua Achebe, *Fragments* by Ayi Kwei Armah, *The River Between* by Ngungi Wa Thiong'o, *God's Bits of Wood* by Sembène Ousmane, and *The Dark Child* by Camara Laye… Thereby, that pre-eminence of African literature in classes has inevitably entailed British literature to be somehow neglected. When it comes to design lesson plans, teachers seldom use novels from British authors such as *Oliver Twist* by Charles Dickens, *Jane Eyre* by Charlotte Brontë, *Heart of Darkness* by Joseph Conrad, etc. It appears that British novels are marginalised in Gabon since teachers seldom use them as language sources for English language acquisition. Thus, the overuse of African literature in classes is problematic since it dramatically shrinks pupils' opportunity to be educated through inputs from other literatures than African literature. That growing imbalance seriously jeopardises pupils' opportunity to develop open-mindness through more than one literature. The trend could be reversed if teachers could use a bit more extracts from British novels during the teaching process. Unquestionably, the use of more than one literature could provide pupils with some more universal educational inputs.

More to the point, it is a fact that English language originates from The United Kingdom. In effect, it is paradoxical that English is not much learned in Gabon through

---

[1] EFL stands for English as a Foreign Language. Usually, this refers to English being taught in a non-English-speaking country but may also refer to any situation where English is being taught to a speaker of another language. An example of EFL is a Gabonese student being taught English in Gabon.

original sources from that country. Teachers should make use of British novels to value the literature of the land where English comes from. The use of British literature could provide teachers with two fundamental advantages. First, British novels constitute authentic sources to English teaching in Gabon, since they are written by native English speakers. Second, as an ancient civilisation, the United Kingdom is rich in social experiences and its literature has inherited such social experiences. That richness can be noticed, for example, in novels from the Victorian Era. These novels were inspired from social unrest in nineteen-century England. Their contents depict and denounce a broad range of social matters. Thus, they are worth using in classes for language acquisition and universal value transmission to pupils.

Seen from that lens, this work proposes *The Mayor of Casterbridge* by Thomas Hardy as an original didactic source for English language acquisition and educational value transmission. That novel was chosen since it had never been used by teachers of English in Gabon and develops interesting topics among which is the consumption of alcohol.

In the light of the above, the topic **"*The Mayor of Casterbridge* for English Acquisition and Anti-Alcohol Sensitisation in Gabon"** is drawn out. This topic is governed by three main aims. Frist, it aims to promote British literature in the teaching of English in Gabon. Second, it aims to provide teachers with authentic language inputs to facilitate pupils' English language acquisition. Third, it aims to use the novel as a means to draw pupils' awareness on the dangerousness of alcohol. On the last aspect evoked, it is not an exaggeration to say that the consumption of alcohol by some Gabonese pupils (a marginal number of them) has become a rampant phenomenon that requires intense sensitisation from parents, educators and authorities.

The problematic can be formulated as follows: How can *The Mayor of Casterbridge* enhance language acquisition and transmit moral values to pupils? We hypothesise that the teachers could exploit its linguistic and social contents to design activities such as debate/discussion, role-play, and dictation to facilitate pupils' English language acquisition while sensitising them to the dangerousness of alcohol. Such activities will be used to help pupils learn English through routine situations of communication in the classroom. Pupils will improve their aural and oral skills through debate/discussion, role-play, and dictation. These activities will make pupils perfectly poised to take more risks to experiment the language they learn. That self-confidence will lead them to practise English outside the classroom, thus facilitating a quicker language acquisition. In addition, the social content of such activities will tremendously help pupils interact over the dangerousness of alcohol. By the means of individual reading and mutual exchanges, learners will develop their critical thinking and self-education on the dangerousness of alcohol. Lastly, the texts and scripts will be used to teach and reinforce other communication skills such as reading and writing, and functional aspects such as vocabulary and grammar. Because that didactic material is written in an advanced English, it will be carefully adjusted to the level of pupils (if necessary).

Coming back to the book under scrutiny, let us say that it recounts the tragedy of Michael Henchard, a man who sells his wife and his baby daughter to a sailor for five guineas because he is inebriated. The teaching activities will be designed around this plot.

The approaches to conduct our demonstration are Language-Based, Theme-Based, and Moral-Philosophical approaches. Learning the language through intensive communication is preponderant in Language-Based approach. Pupils are encouraged to speak and take risks using the language in the classroom. It offers pupils a naturalistic experience of English use and helps develop their ability to practise English on a daily routine outside the classroom. The Theme-Based approach is a way of teaching and learning, whereby many areas of the curriculum are connected and integrated within a theme. In language teaching, it can help to improve the four communication skills and transmit educational values in exploring a theme. The Moral-Philosophical approach consists in equipping pupils with critical reading skills. It enables pupils to draw morality from the reading of a text. It teaches pupils to use their judgement while reading, so that they acquire good behaviour from the reading of the literary text. It favours pupils' self-education and positive personal development. The combination of these three approaches will equip teachers with a framework to reach their teaching objectives.

As far as the selected methods are concerned, it would be worth considering the Direct-Method and Student-centredness. Thanks to the Direct-Method, pupils learn the quickly by speaking no other language than the target language. The memorisation of English spoken sentences accelerates the communicative competence of pupils. Formal inhibition of pupils to use their mother tongue (first language) is favourable for language acquisition, given that pupils are immersed into a naturalistic environment wherein error correction is almost non-existent to give prominence to fluency. As for Student-centredness, let us say that the method favours individual and interactive implications of pupils. Applying it will be beneficial to language acquisition since pupils will rapidly gain knowledge by themselves and from their peers.

This paper encompasses two main interests, scientific and pedagogical. The scientific interest consists in adding a socio-psychological dimension to English language acquisition in Gabon. As for the pedagogical interest, it concerns both teachers and pupils. As far as teachers are concerned, *The Mayor of Casterbridge* will widen their repertoire of English language (re)sources and provide them with supplementary instruments to reinforce anti-drug education in Gabon. As regards pupils, this novel will help spare them from being harmed by alcohol intake. The social content in *The Mayor of Casterbridge* can help them be more studious, responsible, respectful and successful pupils.

This work is articulated around two major parts. The first part is the theoretical framework, which encompasses five chapters. Herein, the key terms of the topic are defined to further clarify its scope. The part also proposes some suitable teaching approaches and methods. Next are the presentation of alcohol consumption by some Gabonese pupils as a social problem that needs to be remedied, articulations of alcohol intake in the novel, and some class activities derived from the novel. The second part comprises three chapters. The first chapter is about data collection and analysis. The second chapter deals with implementation lessons. The last chapter emphasises some difficulties encountered during the investigation and the implementation. It closes with some institutional suggestions.

Literature Review

A few publications related to the relevance of literature in language acquisition and alcohol intake have led to the development of this work. The reader is thus invited to apprehend the following research works

In her article entitled *Teaching Language Through Literature* (2015), Gita Rani Chand asserted that literature is an efficient instrument to teach language areas as grammar, vocabulary and pronunciation, but also to get pupils improve the four communication skills (listening, speaking, reading and writing). In this article, it is claimed that literature is also a rich language teaching instruments whose social content can serve for educational purposes.

In his article entitled *Literature and Language Teaching* (2011), Mundi Rahayu asserted that the aesthetic character of literature is a powerful means for motivation in language classrooms. He considered literature as a powerful teaching source due to its aesthetic representation of social reality, which can motivate pupils to learn by intense implication by seeking meaning while reading and discussing textual contents.

In his article entitled *Teaching Language Through Literature* (2012), T.K Santhi underscored that literature can be used for language acquisition and moral education in language classes. He claimed that literature is more a relevant moral instiling source than some new technologies can be. He stated that literature is always infatuated with cultural and moral content when new technologies may not always provide such aspects. He argued that this cultural content can be leveraged to make learning more attractive and enable a quick language acquisition of pupils.

In their study entitled *Why Should Literature Be Used in Language Classes?* (2012), Nina Davskalovska and Violeta Dimova underscored that literature is worth using in language classes because it provides teachers with a broad range of motivational activities to implicate pupils in their own learning. They think that pupils' critical reading to catch meaning from literary texts can raise omnipresent creativity of pupils and gets the latter to achieve language acquisition the quickest possible.

In his article entitled *Language Acquisition: Acquiring Languages Beyond Knowledge in First Language* (2012), Abena Acheampomaa Darko asserted that language acquisition should derive from motivational factors, because pupils find interest in learning a second language when they are motivated to do that. They think that the attractiveness of the storyline in literature (novels) can be an important factor to draw pupils' attention during language classes.

In 2019, a survey by Yannick Mboumba Sambo showed that 80 percent of teachers he interviewed thought that the level of drug consumption in Gabonese High schools is worrisome. Moreover, 100 percent of those interviewed teachers thought that drug abuse is not suitable for pupils' schooling and success at school (p. 27). These data let us think that drug consumption is an issue that requires to be addressed so far, so as to secure to the Gabonese educative milieu.

In 2013, an article entitled *Health and Social Effects of Alcohol* produced by New Zealander Associate Health Minister Lady Jo Goodhew provided much information on alcohol. In her article, Lady Goodhew criticised the luring pleasure that alcohol can bring to the human being to show that alcohol can be harmful to our body and our brain. Moreover, she asserted that alcohol abuse can make someone lose their rational judgement, personality and common sense.

In her Master's Thesis entitled *The Effect of Alcoholism on Academic Performance of Primary Schools* (2011), Wegosasa Jenepher showed that the consumption of alcoholic drinks can affect pupils mentally and academically. She claims that in Uganda, alcoholism causes many pupils to hardly attend classes or run away from school. Jenepher thinks that the consumption of alcohol by the youth is detrimental for academic pursuits.

In their study entitled *Drugs and School Violence* (2015), Michael Furlong et. al, argued that there is an association between drug use and school violence. In the study, the authors assumed that pupils involved in substance use can engage in high-risk behaviours such as physical aggression or taunting on their schoolmates.

In their study entitled "*The Relationship Between Drinking and Violence in an Adolescent Population: Does Gender Matter?*" (2012), Ronet Bachman and Robert Peralta, asserted that alcohol consumption is one of the most significant factors related to violence and aggression in the youth population. They discovered through their study that the youths who drank heavily were more likely to be not only perpetrators of violence, but also victims of it.

Jane Lilienfeld wrote an article entitled *Alcoholism in the Mayor of Casterbridge* (1999), Therein, she asserted that Hardy's choice to write the tragedy of an alcoholic man who decides to abstain from drinking alcohol is a narrative strategy to encourage abstinence. She adds that the narrative strategy Hardy used is indicative of his desire to get his Victorian readers to practise abstinence to alcohol. She draws a parallel between Hardy's biography and the novel to compare Hardy's father (who had drinking problems) with Michael Henchard, the protagonist. Lilienfeld thinks that Hardy created

Michael Henchard as an alcoholic character to emphasise the harmfulness of alcohol on his own family.

In 2021, Ralph Obandja Boyo's work demonstrated that *A Christmas Carol* by Charles Dickens could be used as an authentic didactic (re) source to help pupils achieve language acquisition and moral value transmission.

In her Master's Thesis entitled *Teaching English Through Some African Literary Texts to Improve Pupils' Language Acquisition: The Case of the Second Cycle*, Mareille Eyang (2020) explained that the use of African literary texts can help to improve pupils' language acquisition and develop their communicative skills. She equally stated that these literary texts were useful to teach some African culture and values.

Part One: Theoretical Framework

Introduction of Part One

The first chapter brings clarifying information on the key terms of the topic. The second chapter proposes some suitable teaching approaches and methods to teach English through *The Mayor of Casterbridge*. The third chapter is devoted to showing alcohol intake as a rampant phenomenon in Gabonese schools. In fact, this chapter highlights some major factors responsible for that phenomenon and shows how governmental and nongovernmental actions intend to remedy alcohol intake at pupils'. The fourth chapter develops the theme of alcoholism leaning on some striking episodes from the novel. The fifth chapter proposes some interactive activities destined to show how *The Mayor of Casterbridge* can be used in English classes.

Chapter I: Clarification of Key-Terms

This chapter is about the clarification of the key terms surrounding the topic. These are *Thomas Hardy, The Mayor of Casterbridge, Authentic Source, Language Acquisition, Alcohol,* and *Sensitisation*. The respective definitions of these terms will be helpful for the reader's clear understanding of the topic.

I.1. Thomas Hardy

The presentation of Thomas Hardy is critical to the understanding of our topic. As the author of the book under study, it is fundamental for the reader to have information concerning his biography and bibliography.

I.1.1. Biography

Born on 2 June 1840 in Stinsford, Dorset (England), Thomas Hardy was an English novelist and poet. At the age of eight, he attended school. However, most of his education came from books. Teaching himself, he learned French, German and Latin. When he was 16, he became apprentice to a local architect named John Hicks. Aged 22, he went to London to work with architect Arthur Blomfield, and immersed himself in the cultural scene.

On the literary ground, Hardy began writing poetry that idealised rural life, but could not find a publisher. He left London in 1867. In the course of the same year, he entered a temporary engagement with Tryphena Sparks, a sixteen-year-old relative (*Masterpiece*, 2016, p. 1).

Not finding an audience for his poetry, novelist George Meredith advised Hardy to write a novel. Accordingly, he wrote *The Poor Man and the Lady*, but publishers rejected it, and he destroyed the manuscript. Hardy's first popular novel, *Under the Greenwood Tree* (1872), marked the beginning of his career as a famous novelist. He used to write anonymously, but as his popularity considerably increased, he finally used his own name. Like Dickens's, Hardy's novels were published in serial form in magazines. He died on January 11, 1928, aged eighty-seven years old, in Dorchester, England.

I.1.2. A Selected Bibliography

Throughout his literary career, Thomas Hardy penned many novels. The most well known of them include:

Under the Greenwood Tree (1872): This novel is Hardy's second novel to be published. He became a well-known novelist thanks to that masterpiece. The plot unfolds in the small village of Mellstock in Thomas Hardy's fictional Wessex. It is about a love story and the disappearance of old traditions (move toward a more modern way of life).

A Pair of Blue Eyes (1873): This novel is about the story of Elfride Swancourt, a vicar's daughter living in a remote corner of England, who is forced to choose between two very different men. The first suitor, Stephen Smith, is a young architect whom she meets when he is sent by his employer to survey the church building. The second suitor, Henry Knight, once Stephen's mentor, is a barrister and an editor.

The Mayor of Casterbridge (1886): This novel is one of Hardy's most dramatic works of fiction. This fictitious epitomization of Victorian England was highly successful. It has been adapted many times into cinematography. Furthermore, the book portrays a certain poor hay-trusser Micheal Henchard, who quits poverty and becomes the wealthy mayor of the small town of Casterbridge. Being the book under study, it will be thoroughly developed in the next section.

'*Jude the Obscure*' (1895) is known as Hardy's masterpiece. It tells the story of a working-class young man from southern England, Jude Fawley, who dreams of becoming a scholar at the prestigious university at Christminster, modelled on the world-famous Oxford University. Before this can happen, however, Jude is tricked into marriage by the seductive, but opportunistic, Arabella Donn, who falsely claims she is pregnant. The marriage soon falls apart and Jude travels to Christminster, only to be denied entry to the university. The classical studies he has pursued all his life, almost entirely on his own, have been in vain. As a result, he has neither the education, nor the money to become a scholar.

The Well-Beloved (1897): Published in 1897, *The Well-Beloved* is the closing novel of the Wessex novels series and the last novel penned by Hardy. The novel tells the story of the sculptor Jocelyn Pierston's search for the ideal woman, through three generations of a Portland family.

I.2. The Mayor of Casterbridge

I.2.1. Background, Context, and Category of the Book

The Mayer of Casterbridge: The Life and Death of a Man of Character is known as Thomas Hardy's eighth novel. It was first published in two volumes in 1886. Strictly speaking, before it became a novel, it had been a novella. That is, the book had been published in the form of a serial of episodes in a Journal called *The Graphic* (1885).

The Mayor of Casterbridge was written in the Victorian England context. That is why the book is rich in textual representations referring to the Victorian Age. Furthermore, the book is categorised in the Victorian realistic novel, a kind of novel written with journalistic techniques to be closer to real-life. The realistic novel has the particularity to emphasise facts and general stereotypes of human nature (Hainer, 2017, p. 2). The Victorian realistic novel depicts Victorian England social realities such as the Industrial Revolution, women's precarious social condition, child abuse, prostitution, poverty, proletariat life, social class warfare, urban insecurity, and urban insalubrity, to name a few (Weston, 2021, pp. 1-12).

I.2.2. Characterisation

After presenting the background of the novel, its literary context, and its category, let us now turn to the presentation of its characters. There are eight central characters in *The Mayor of Casterbridge*. They are presented in order of importance as follows:

Micheal Henchard: Henchard is the towering but tragic hero in the story. At the beginning, he is a twenty-one-year-old English hay-trusser in the quest for a job. He sells his wife and daughter in an auction sale because he is drunk. Eighteen years later he becomes a rich merchant in the fictitious town of Casterbridge and the mayor of that small country town.

Donald Farfrea: A young Scottish man who arrives in the city of Casterbridge at about the same time as Susan and Elizabeth-Jane. He quickly becomes Henchard's only trusted friend. Later, he becomes Henchard's adversary in both business and love.

Susan Henchard: Susan Henchard is Michael Henchard's wife as the novel opens. Hardy portrays her as being naïve and resigned to an existence over which she is powerless. In the storyline her husband, Michael Henchard sells her to a sailor named Richard Newson. Later in the storyline, she is referred to as Susan Newson.

Elizabeth-Jane Enchard: This name is associated with two different characters in the book. Firstly, it refers to the baby daughter of Michael and Susan Henchard who dies after her father [Henchard] sells them to Richard Newson. Secondly, it refers to the grown-up girl that returns to Casterbridge alongside with Susan to search Henchard eighteen years later. The narrator reveals that she is not the daughter of Micheal Henchard but Susan and Newson's daughter. Her real name is Elizabeth-Jane Newson.

The furmity Saleswoman: An old saleswoman who sells furmity in the fun fair. She runs the shop in which Michael Henchard gets drunk and sells his wife. Later in the storyline, as an eyewitness, she testifies before a judge that Henchard sold his wife during a trial against him.

Mr Richard Newson: The sailor who buys Susan and Elizabeth-Jane at the beginning of the storyline. He is the father of Elisabeth-Jane Newson.

Lucetta Templeman: She is a superficial woman who, like Henchard, suffers several reversals of fortune and ends badly. Henchard has an affair with her before Susan arrives in Casterbridge.

Jopp: A lowlife villain driven by dark emotions. He dislikes Farfrea because Henchard hired Farfrea as the manager of his company in his stead.

I.2.3. Plot

The Mayor of Casterbridge narrates the story of a twenty-one-year-old English hay-trusser named Michael Henchard. During a job-trip he undertakes from a rural area to the small country town of Casterbridge, Michael Henchard decides to halt at a fair alongside his wife, Susan and their baby daughter, Elizabeth-Jane. They decide to halt with intent to rest for a while and have breakfast before they pursue their way as far as the town of Casterbridge. After they start to eat their basins of porridge, Michael decides to order some liquor, which he pours into his basin of furmity porridge. Shortly after he has drunk four full basins of rum, Micheal becomes orally and emotionally aggressive toward his wife. Prompted by the liquor, he accuses her of being the source of his financial misery. Thus, he decides to get rid of her by selling her in an auction for five guineas sum.

In the early morning, Henchard recovers sobriety. After he learns that he has sold his beloved ones because he was drunk, Henchard scolds himself for that disgraceful deed and swears to abstain from drinking alcohol for a twenty-one-year timespan. Then, he decides to carry on his trip to the town of Casterbridge to start a new life. Eighteen years later, Henchard is evoked as a respected and admired rich corn merchant and the mayor of the town of Casterbridge. He is esteemed for his acute sense of business and his sobriety. He lives a life of stability and remarries with Susan until she dies. Shortly after Susan's death, Henchard experiences bankruptcy and breaks the oath of abstinence from alcohol. The loss of his position of power suddenly leads him to drink much, ridicule himself publicly, and antagonise many people in his entourage. As a result, that tumultuous demeanour of Henchard causes people such as Farfrea and

Elizabeth-Jane to treat him scornfully. Haunted with shame, he thus decides to leave the town of Casterbridge to live in seclusion in a dirty, miserable, and small cottage at a village not far from Casterbridge. Thereby, Michael dies in the most unbearable miserable conditions.

I.2.4. Setting and Time

The narration is set in the fictitious town of Casterbridge, located in Wessex, a fictitious borough in Eastern England. Hardy made a mixture of an ancient-time England kingdom's name with the features of nineteen-century Dorset borough. For example, Hardy's Wessex has a lot of modernity-related features such as elegant houses, city hall, hotels, inns, fun fairs... However, the real Wessex that used to exist referred to the medieval world's setting.

As far as time is concerned, the narration in the novel is temporally related to Victorian Age[2]. We can notice that the storyline in the book evokes social issues that took place at that landmark historic and literary period. As regards the originality and the interesting sociocultural content in *The Mayor of Casterbridge*, this book may be considered as an authentic source to enable English language acquisition at pupils'.

I.3. Authentic Source

The definitions of authentic materials are slightly different in literature by different researchers of language. Harmer (1991, p. 25) defines authentic texts as *"materials such as books, newspapers, videos, and audios which are designed for native speakers; they are real cultural materials designed not for language students, but for the native speakers of the language"*. Jordan (1997, p. 34) refers to authentic texts as *"texts that are not written for language teaching purposes"*. Peacock (1997, p. 84) describes authentic materials as "*materials that have been produced to fulfil some social purpose in the language community"*. What we understand that is common in these definitions is that authentic materials offer students *"some exposure to real language and opportunity to use it as done in its own community"* (Widdoson, 1990, p. 27). In other words, it is the benefit that students get from being exposed to the language in authentic materials. In short, in an E.F.L context, *"authentic materials are materials that we can use with the students in the classroom and that have not been*

---

[2] It is a period of British history symbolised by Queen Victorian's rule in the nineteen centuries. But its influence in literature continued until the early twentieth century. It is a period when there had been tremendous social, scientific and literary upheavals.

changed in any way for ESL students. A classic example would be a newspaper article that is written for a native-English-speaking audience" (Sanderson, 1999, p. 13).

Using authentic material in the classroom may be significant for many reasons. First, learners are exposed to real discourse, as in videos of interviews with famous people. They may provide learners with exposure to real language. Second, the originality of the socio-cultural content in authentic materials may have a positive effect on learners' motivation. The sociocultural content of authentic materials may appeal to learners' interest and enhance their motivation to learn the target language. Third, authentic materials may keep learners informed about what is happening in the world, so that they have an intrinsic educational value. Last but not the least, authentic materials support a more creative approach to teaching by eliciting interactions in the language classroom (Tamo, 2009, pp. 2-3). As regards all these advantages they may bring into the language classroom, authentic materials should be extensively used so to facilitating language acquisition at learners'. In the context of this Master's Thesis research paper, the proposed authentic material is Thomas Hardy's *The Mayor of Casterbridge*, a British literature masterpiece.

I.4. Language Acquisition

The task consisting in clarifying the *Language acquisition concept* requires the terms *language* and *acquisition* to be defined separately. A *language* is defined in the *Collins Cobuild English Language Dictionary* (1992, p. 809) as *"a system of communication which consists of set of sounds and written symbols which are used by the people of a particular country or region for talking or writing"*. In other words, it is a system of signs, codes, images, and symbols that allow men in a specific human community to express ideas, feelings, thoughts, philosophy, etc.

As regards *acquisition*, the *Collins Cobuild English Language Dictionary* (p. 12) defines this term to be *"the cognitive process of acquiring skill or knowledge"*. Acquisition refers to gaining, or getting a package of knowledge, abilities, competences or expertise. It is an intellectual process that permits someone to access a certain degree of information. Corroboratively, the *Longman Online Dictionary* states that *acquisition* is *"the process by which you knowledge or learn a skill"*. This corroboration testifies the universality of the clarification one has of the term *acquisition*. As far as language learning is concerned, *language acquisition* is the intellectual process through which language learners can attain a near-native performance in using a target language to communicate (Saville-Stroike, 2006, p. 4). For the case of this study, the targeted language is English.

I.5. Alcohol

The *Collins Cobuild English Language Dictionary* (p. 34) defines *alcohol* as being *"drinks such as beer, wine and whiskey that make people drunk"*. The term *alcohol* plays a prominent role in the framework of this research paper. This term is related to the novel that is on the core of our dissertation. In effect, some articulations related to alcohol intake from the book will help to demonstrate how *The Mayor of Casterbridge* can prevent Gabonese pupils from being the victims of the side effects of alcohol intake in many respects. The term *alcohol* appears in this work not to be eulogised, but to be pilloried as a rampant social phenomenon that threatens the safe schooling of Gabonese pupils. Thus, *The Mayor of Casterbridge* is proposed as an educational instrument to remedy the problem of alcohol consumption by Gabonese pupils.

I.6. Sensitisation.

Sensitisation is a noun that derives from the verb *sensitise*. According to the *Collins Cobuild English Language Dictionary* (p. 1316), *"if you sensitise people to a particular problem or situation, you make them aware of it"*. In other words, sensitisation consists in raising people's awareness on the dangerousness a something bad to their safety.

In teaching, in addition to knowledge transmission to pupils, teachers are recommended to use didactic materials as instruments to sensitise the latter on various social matters. In this context, *sensitisation* might be viewed as a synonym of *prevention*. The *Collins Cobuild English Language Dictionary* affirms that preventive actions *"are intended to help stop negative things such as disease or crimes from occurring"* (p. 1337). Therefore, teaching becomes a preventive instrument with intent to raise pupils' awareness, so to spare them from being harmed by such social matters. In short, sensitisation in schools resides in teachers' skilfulness in using didactic materials such as texts, videos, and audios to educate pupils. Therefore, our research work presents *The Mayor Casterbridge* as an instrument to sensitise pupils to the dangerousness of alcohol intake in Gabonese high schools.

Chapter II: Some Suitable Approaches and Methods to Enable Language Acquisition and Sensitise to the Dangerousness of Alcohol Intake at Pupils'

This chapter emphasises the different teaching approaches and methods that can best suit the implementation of *The Mayor of Casterbridge* for English language acquisition and sensitisation to the dangerousness of alcohol.

II.1. Suitable Approaches to Encourage Interaction and Self-Moral Education at Pupils'

Three approaches will be the focus of this section. These are: Language-based, Theme-based, and Moral Philosophical approaches. They have been selected because of their relevance to our study.

II.1.1. Language-Based Approach

Language-based approach refers to applying the communicative approach to the use of literary texts in language teaching. The Language-Based Approach is the teaching approach that best suits the use of literary texts to teach English language in the classroom. The paramount objective of language-based approach is language acquisition through classroom activities derived from the study of a literary text. This approach particularly attaches much importance to using the content of the literary text to facilitate pupils' language acquisition through intensive practice on the four basic communication skills. Thus, in that approach communication is more a means to learn a language than it is an objective to attain. In other words, the language-based approach gives more prominence to realistic communication situations for pupils to be using the target language as a daily routine so that *in fine* they reach a near-native performance and competence.

Pupils should use a literary text with the ultimate aim of linguistic practice rather than solely reading literature to obtain facts and information as regards Language–Based approach (Savvidou, 2011, p. 32). Thus, language-based approach puts stress on the interest of using a literary text to improve the functional aspects of the language in pupils. The content (the storyline, themes, or morality) in the literary text becomes as the basement on which skill-improving activities will be designed with a view to improve pupils' language communicative skills and their achievement of communicative performance. In fact, the aim of this approach is to convert the content (either cultural, social, or scientific) of a literary text into a teaching instrument with intent to supply pupils with naturalistic circumstances of target language use.

Applying this approach leads to see the use of literature as a vehicle through which the four skills of English language can be improved by designing activities intended to encourage interaction, pair-working, group-working and interdependence among pupils. The approach requires the content in the text to be attractive for pupils to be motivated and actively participate to English language learning drilling (Rahman, 2016, p. 158). The teacher can use the content of the literary text to design communication skills improving activities such as role-playing, group debate, dual debate, storytelling, discussion groups, dialogues, singing and even poetry. These activities are motivating, and they encourage pupils to be creative during language classes, that is, they help develop the four skills of pupils by making them self-confident to be talkative and poised to take risks in using the language they learn. Febriani et. al give an overall view on Language-Based approach as follows:

> *Related to the purpose of using literature in EFL classroom in the attempt to improve the students' English proficiency, Van (2009) has also analysed an approach that emphasizes on developing the students' language skill, which is called Language-based approach. This approach emphasizes the awareness of the language of literature which is a basic stage for EFL learners. Van believed that the approach is more accessible for language learners since it facilitates the students' responses and experience with literature. Language-based approach provides a variety of language instruction activities. Literature is seen as an excellent vehicle resulting in the four skills of English language development through interaction, collaboration, peer teaching, and student interdependence. The role of the teacher, therefore, is to introduce and clarify technical terms, to prepare and offer appropriate classroom procedures, and to intervene when necessary to provide prompts or stimuli. Language-based approach to teaching literature offers the opportunity for students to improve their English proficiency through literary works.* (2018, p. 41)

Language-Based Approach leads the teacher to design activities with aim of the integration of skills in pupils. In such activities, the four skills should be linked so far. Thus, each skill is not taught as an isolated unit. There is a correlation between the four skills. It means that the improvement of one skill should entail the improvement of the other skills. For instance, speaking performance could result from listening, reading, or writing activities.

In short, Language-Based approach enables teachers to teach listening, speaking, reading and writing through activities which derive from the comprehension process of a literary text. These activities are expected to bring near-native experience of English use into the classroom to accustom pupils with handling the communicative skills and acquire the language the quickest possible.

II.1.2. Theme-Based Approach

Some experts describe Theme-Based as an approach to language teaching in which the whole course is structured around certain themes or topics (Brinton, 2001). Theme-Based teaching (also termed theme-based instruction or topic-based teaching) is one of the approaches with the broader model of Content-Based instruction in which the emphasis is on exposing students to a *"highly contextualized"* second language environment by using the subject matter as the content of language learning.

Theme-based instruction defends very well the principle of *"integration"*. According to Richards and Rodgers (Richards and Rodgers, 1986, p. 101), themes or topics promote continuity and coherence across skill areas and focus on using language in connected discourse rather than isolated pieces of language. In this sense, theme-based courses bring together knowledge, language and thinking skills.

In a Theme-Based course, different teaching activities are integrated by their content, the teaching of different skill areas is incorporated into the theme, and "the theme or topic acts as a connecting thread. The rationale for this thematic approach is to *"avoid fragmentation and unconnected skill exercise*s" and through a variety of activities, it provides learners with motivating and meaningful uses of the language.

Other important advantages of Theme-Based Teaching for language learning as suggested by Cameron include the fact that new vocabulary items can be learned easily, with the theme providing a meaningful context for understanding, and for the natural use of a wide range of discourse types, both written and spoken (p. 16).

II.1.3. Moral-Philosophical Approach

We consider the basic position of literary critics such as Samuel Johnson who asserts that the larger function of literature is to teach morality and probe philosophical and even sociological issues. This standing point indicates that literature in its essence has a teaching function. Thus, it is an adequate instrument to transmit values in general. Matthew Arnold claimed that a great literature must have a *"high seriousness"* (Guerin et al., 2005, p. 75). This utterance by Arnold let us think that all issues which literature deals with, have a serious tone. It aims to state that there are positive messages encoded in literature intended to teach serious moral values. This means that literature has a paramount role to play in education toward teaching pupils those moral values.

In the language teaching context, the moral-philosophical approach is the adequate approach toward teaching literature in its educative function. This approach incorporates the fact of conveying moral values across the curriculum[3]. The focus of this approach is to make pupils discover universal humanistic values while they are reading a literary text. In other words, it seeks to make pupils find the worthiness and considerations of applying critical thinking to draw morality from their individual reading of a literary text (Dweikat and Shbeitah, 2014, p. 19).

Besides, let us consider the preceding standing point to understand that philosophy is an important area in moral-philosophical approach. It mostly has the meaning of critical thinking in this context. Indeed, reading presents students with facts. Students are expected to think over these facts for them to have a critical opinion over these facts. The objective is to make pupils acquire moral values through their own thinking and interaction with their classmates over the topic.

In addition, the approach thus appeals pupils to self-education through literature. It appeals for students to share moral values with their entourage. Consequently, we also notice that the Moral-Philosophical approach has a sociological scope. This sociological scope resides in the fact that literature deals with real-life social matters. It also resides in the fact that interaction during class activities enables pupils to debate over such matters to mutually educate one another.

In moral-philosophical approach pupils acquire educational information from the text for themselves and from their peers. Thus, this approach instils an environment of mutual moral education among pupils in the language class. They are immersed in an environment wherein they convey moral values to one another. In such an environment, they learn the virtuousness of having a good deportment in everyday life.

Thus, applying the Moral-Philosophical approach to the teaching of *The Mayor of Casterbridge* might be helpful. It might lead pupils to draw, from this novel, the necessary moral information for them to be aware of the dangerousness of alcohol intake. Not only will pupils draw educative morality from individual reading of that book, but they will also get such educational inputs from their peers. That mutual education at pupils' will depend on interactive activities such as discussion groups, debate, and role-play, to name a few. For instance, these activities might be based on the dangerousness of alcohol based on *Michael Henchard's wife sale due to his*

---

[3] This approach goes beyond language teaching. It means that class activities are not restricted to language acquisition; it also dedicated to teaching humanistic values to students. It utilises the English class to entice pupils to have a critical thinking about coming social matters happening in their social environment.

inebriety to create an environment whereby pupils go deep into that topic to sensitise one another to the dangerousness of such a phenomenon.

II.2. Some Suitable Methods to Facilitate Language Acquisition at Pupils'

For the purpose of our work, we have identified two appropriate methods, namely, Student-Centredness and the Direct Method. Below are the reasons for their suitability.

II.2.1. Student-Centredness

The student-centred learning approach is diametrically opposed to the philosophy underlying the conventional method of learning[4] (Attard et al., 2010, p. 9). By its very nature, student-cantered learning allows students to shape their own learning paths and places upon them the responsibility to actively participate in making their educational process a meaningful one.

By definition, the student-centred learning experience is not a passive one, as it is based on the premise that 'student passivity does not support or enhance learning' and that it is precisely 'active learning' which helps students to learn independently (MacHemer and Crawford, p. 11). Within Student-centredness, students are given options in shaping their courses and in choosing particular units within their study programme. Some proponents of student centredness assert that rather than devoting so much effort to teaching students what to think, SCL is based on the idea of teaching them how to think' (Tsui, 2002, p. 740).

Furthermore, within student-cantered learning there is an intrinsic motivation for learning, with the emphasis being on cooperation, rather than competition, between students. As part of this approach students are given the opportunity to compare their ideas with their peers and their teachers while contributing to developing their curricula in a meaningful manner.

In this context, the student is encouraged to ask questions and be inquisitive and the academic is seen as a facilitator and guide, rather than as the main source of knowledge. This approach therefore changes the role of the teacher, from being

---

[4] Conventional learning considers students as passive receptors of information, without consideration of the need to actively participate in the learning process. Within the conventional approach to learning, curricular design is based on low levels of student participation, as decisions in the learning process revolve around the privileged position of the academic as students' main source of knowledge. Indeed, it is a non-participatory approach, where students are rarely expected to ask questions or to challenge the theories of the academic.

entrusted with the 'transmission of knowledge to supporting and guiding self-regulated student learning' (Van Eekelen et al., 2005, p. 447).

II.2.2. The Direct-Method

The Direct Method was the outcome of a reaction against the Grammar-Translation Method. The Grammar-Translation Method offered very little beyond an insight into the grammatical rules attending the process of translating from the second to the native language (Richards and Rodgers, p. 88). The Grammar-Translation Method was simply associated with mere rote memorisation of parts of the speech and learning grammar rules in order for learners to translate second language literature into the first language. The defect with that Method is its inefficiency in facilitating language acquisition, because it does not give prominence to oral interaction in the target langue.

Compared to the Grammar-Translation Method, the Direct Method assumes that the learner of a foreign language should be given instruction, think, and express directly in the target language. So, to speak, according to this method English is taught through English. The learners acquire English through discussion, conversation, and reading solely in English. As a matter of fact, the Direct Method does not take recourse to translation into learners' first language (Alkhateeb, 2011, p. 1).

In addition, the Direct Method aims to establish the direct bond between thought and expression as well as between experience and language. In other words, the method allows students to practise English in real-life condition of communication. Instructions in class activities are given solely in English by the teacher so as for students to listen, speak, read and write English without taking recourse to the first language of the learners.

In fact, the sole use of English arouses the instinctive language sense in the students (Alkhateeb, p. 2). That inner instinctive language sense which every human being possesses in their first language supersedes all rules, grammar and dictionaries. It allows for language acquisition through the direct association between experience and expression. This direct experience with English ensures immediate and instinctive acquisition of that target language.

Moreover, the Direct method's aim of target language acquisition through direct experience is a well-structured method which obeys to several principles, as follows:

Prominence of oral training: Emphasis is put on oral training through the listening-speaking relationship. That is, the students are given sufficient practice in listening to the language and then are commended to speak it. Thus, such activities help provide students with authentic phonetic and pronunciation of the target language. Oral training establishes direct association between words of the target language and the idea for which they stand.

Inhibition of the mother tongue: Any use of students' first language or mother tongue is inhibited during class activities. Students are taught new words by actually showing them the objects for which they stand or by performing actions and suitable illustration in context.

The sentence is the smallest unit of speech: The teaching of a language starts with the teaching of sentence patterns rather than individual words. This enables the learner to internalise the structure of the target language. New vocabulary items are introduced gradually based on the principle of selection and gradation. They are taught through material association, explanation or used in suitable context.

Inductive teaching of grammar: In the direct method, grammar of the target language is not taught for its own sake as usual. It is a means to an end. That is, it aims to enable every student to correct errors in their speech and writing for themselves (Alkhateeb, p. 2).

In short, the Direct Method is a highly practical method for language acquisition. It is based on the use of direct experience to help learners acquire the target language. On its core are oral activities and total physical response or illustration. The relation between oral training and physical total response helps students grab the target language meaning of objects, moods, actions, facts with no recourse to translation.

The Direct-Method intends to grant much importance to pupils' thinking. In fact, it is peculiar for inhibiting the use of the first language. It aims at sparing pupils from translating inputs in their mind before they give answers to these inputs in a conversation. If pupils can think in the target language, and if they do not translate in their mind, they will gain fluency and attain near-native performance the quickest possible.

Thus, implementing the Direct Methods would help teachers to accelerate the language acquisition of pupils. *In fine*, it can be stated that the Direct-Method is a suitable method to develop the functional aspect of language learning, which is the ability to communicate in the target language. In sum, we selected these approaches and methods for their ability to arouse interaction and offer intensive communicative practice. These approaches were chosen we intent to help demonstrate how *The Mayor of Casterbridge* can facilitate the English language acquisition and sensitise to the dangerousness of alcohol intake at pupils'.

Chapter III: The Consumption of Alcohol: A Rampant Phenomenon in Gabon

> *Le Gabon vient, une fois de plus, de confirmer sa place de leader continental en terme de consommation d'alcool. Ce positionnement en champion d'Afrique de consommation d'alcool a été révélé par l'Organisation Mondiale de la Santé (OMS), via son rapport d'enquête sur la question.*[5]

The above quote is an alarming indicator that gives one the gist of the present chapter. To be more specific, this chapter points out alcohol intake as a plaguing phenomenon, which dramatically affects the safety and the good schooling of pupils in Gabon. Herein, the main factors behind that rampant phenomenon are highlighted. The chapter closes with the presentation of the main actors involved in the fight against alcohol intake by pupils and their respective methods to remedy that rampant phenomenon as well.

III.1. Synopsis: Harmful Effects of Alcohol Consumption by Pupils

Alcohol consumption is a social issue, which affects pupils in Gabon. The consumption of alcohol also entails pupils to be victims of many other universal social problems susceptible to threaten their lives and their studies. Firstly, alcohol consumption may entail risky sexual behaviour at pupils'. Minors who drink alcohol more commonly engage in sexual intercourse shortly after drinking and have sexual experiences at an earlier age. They may have sex with multiple partners and engage in unprotected or unplanned sex intercourse. This may lead them to experience unexpected pregnancies, and contract sexually transmitted diseases and infections such as HIV/Aids and gonorrhoea, to name a few (Hanes, 2012, p. 5).

Secondly, alcohol intake can dramatically impact pupils' academic performance. Underage drinkers may miss classes, become inefficient in their schoolwork, earn lower grades, and perform poorly on examinations and assignments. They may also drop out, fail classes, or be expelled from school (p. 7). Last but not the least, alcohol intake may entail accidental injuries and alcohol-related death at minors and young adults. Alcohol can put pupils in dangerous situations that may cause pupils to be victims of life-threatening accidents, including drowning, burns, and falls (p. 6). Outside the school fence, alcohol consumption may engender pupil-on-pupil physical and emotional violence such as stabbing, fighting, robbery, mockery, insulting, and

---

[5] LANNA, *Ethique Media Gabon*, 2022. *Gabon has once again confirmed its position as the continental leader in terms of alcohol consumption. This position as Africa's champion of alcohol consumption was revealed by the World Health Organization (WHO), via its investigation report on the issue.*

raping. It can equally involve pupils in traffic accidents. Pupils can get hurt and killed by fast driving cars while attempting to walk across highways in a drunken mood.

Attending classes while they are drunk, some pupils lose their concentration or sleep. Some others disturb classes by uttering impolite jokes in presence of the teacher. Such a situation may lead to class interruption. For instance, in 2010, in Lambaréné, two drunken fifth-form pupils from Charles Mefane High School vomited in the classroom and provoked some disturbance at their classmates'. That situation led the teacher to interrupt the History and Geography lesson. Thus, the consumption of alcohol by pupils can disturb teaching and learning activities. It can negatively affect both pupils and teachers.

Browsing through social media, online news media, or even through television, people have recurrently read, heard, or watched cases of definitive exclusions of drunk pupils at school. That phenomenon happens countrywide. For instance, in October 2021, in the hinterland town of Ndéndé (Ngounié Province), two drunken pupils were permanently excluded from Paul Marie Yembit High School. *Gabonews* (2021) breaks the news:

> *Deux élèves de 4e du lycée d'État de Ndendé, dans la province de la Ngounié (sud du Gabon), ont été définitivement exclus de leur établissement suite à la décision du directoire de cet établissement, pour cas d'indiscipline avérée et de consommation de boissons alcoolisées pendant les de cours a-t-on appris de la télévision locale Lowa TV.*
> *Selon cette source d'information, les deux élèves du lycée d'état Paul Marie Yembit de Ndendé se sont présentés aux cours dans un état d'ébriété en début de semaine, perturbant les enseignements, avec ce que cela comporte comme désagréments pour les autres élèves et les enseignants.*
> *Pour Mr Moussavou, proviseur du lycée d'état de Ndendé, il n'est pas question de faire preuve d'indulgence à ce sujet (…)*
> *Les deux compères ont donc été définitivement exclus de l'établissement, bien que voulant à tout prix se justifier, tout en implorant la clémence des responsables qui ont été fermes sur leur position*[6]

The cases of these two unluckily excluded pupils prove that the consumption of alcohol by pupils dramatically jeopardises their schooling. As regards the conduct rules

---

[6] Two fourth grade students from the state high school of Ndendé, in Ngounié Province (southern Gabon), were definitively excluded from their establishment following the decision of the management board of this establishment, for cases of proven indiscipline and consumption of alcoholic beverages during lessons, we learned from local television Lowa TV. According to this source of information, the two students of Paul Marie Yembit high school in Ndendé showed up for lessons in a drunken state at the start of the week, disrupting the lessons, with what this entails as inconvenience for others. Students and teachers. For Mr Moussavou, headmaster of the Ndendé state high school, there is no question of being indulgent on this subject (...). The two accomplices were therefore permanently excluded from the establishment. Although they wanted to justify themselves at all costs, those in charge remained firm in their position.

in Gabonese schools, drinking alcohol and being in a drunken mood at school is a misbehaviour that deserves a disciplinary sanction. Pupils who act so reprehensibly at school must be presented before the disciplinary council of the school to undergo a punishment proportional to their misbehaviour. That punishment may range from a warning, blame, temporary exclusion, to a definitive exclusion from the school. Thus, alcohol consumption is quite dangerous for pupils because it might be a cause of school dropouts.

The definitive exclusion might be applied as a sanction to the disciplinary defects of pupils at school, but it is applied exceptionally in the most serious cases of pupils' misconduct.

It is evident that alcohol prompts pupils to misbehave at school. Most of the time such pupils are punished. We can ascertain that punishment is somehow necessary in education, but too much severe punishment tends to mean that pupils are the sole responsible for their indiscipline and misconduct, which are sometimes linked to alcohol intake. Pupils are mostly the victims of that phenomenon since they are impelled to drink alcohol due to some exogenous factors.

III.2. Some Factors Inherent to Alcohol Intake by Pupils

The fraudulent nearness of dinking bars, the inexistent adulthood checks to enter these bars, and the omnipresence of alcohol advertising billboard near schools are some of the main causes of the consumption of alcohol by pupils in Gabon. The proximity of drinking bars and alcohol advertising billboards to schools and the cupidity of bar tenders prompt pupils to drink alcoholic drinks precociously and enter the school fence while they are drunk. Some pupils even dare to break the school regulations by coming into the classroom while they are in a drunken mood. As a result, such pupils most often expose themselves to the punishments provided in the regulations inherent to correcting misbehaviour of pupils at school.

III.2.1. Bar Activities near Schools

In Gabon, many bar owners overtly break the Decree No 0408/PR/MISPID of July 1, 2012. This decree enforced by the Gabonese government strictly forbids bars and other alcohol-selling establishments to be located less than two hundred metres (200 m) from public or private schools on the whole Gabonese territory. The aim of this decree is to protect pupils and ensure their safe schooling.

Despite the decree is already enforced, it is recurrent to remark that many drinking bars are located near public and private secondary schools countrywide. Sometimes, such alcohol selling enterprises are even located beside the fence of some secondary schools. As a matter of fact, here in Libreville City, we can name a few examples of the kind. We can immediately evoke the cases of schools such as Ntchoréré, Quaben, Colbert, Léon MBA, la Réussite High Schools and Frère Macaire Junior High School. All these secondary schools are surrounded with alcohol selling businesses such as bars, pubs or beer warehouses. Alix-Ida Mussavu from *Gabonreview* corroborates that viewpoint in her 2019 report:

> *Dans un communiqué rendu public ce 4 novembre, le ministère de l'Intérieur informe l'opinion et particulièrement les tenanciers des débits de boissons situés aux abords des établissements scolaires que « les Forces de police nationale procèderont dans les tout prochains jours, à la fermeture, et le cas échéant, au déguerpissement desdits commerces ». Pour ainsi dire, par arrêté n°52 du 1er octobre 2019, Edgard Anicet Mboumbou Miyakou avait ordonné la fermeture des débits de boissons installés aux abords des établissements scolaires sur l'ensemble du territoire national.*[7]

That situation is problematic. These alcohol selling businesses are fraudulently located near schools since they do not comply with governmental policies, which forbid all bar activities near schools. First, the music they play loudly may disturb the quietness needed for pupils to learn. It is played on purpose to attract adolescent people so that they would consume alcoholic drinks. However, most pupils are not yet adorned with the necessary maturity to avoid entering bars and drinking alcohol. As adolescent people, pupils are very curious to experiment good or bad things when they are far from their homes. Thus, the presence of drinking bars near the schools where they attend classes most of the time exposes them to start drinking alcohol before and after classes.

III.2.2. Lack of Strict Adulthood Check to Enter Drinking Places

Despite the government's effort to forbid all minors people and pupils wearing a school uniform from buying alcoholic drinks, or even entering alcohol selling places, the tenders of these drinking places are still selling alcohol to pupils. They even let pupils in without any rigorous adulthood check. Of course, these bar tenders know that letting minors enter drinking bars is a felony that dramatically endangers their studies

---

[7] In a press release made public on November 4, the Ministry of the Interior informs the public and particularly the owners of drinking establishments located near schools that 'the National Police Forces will proceed in the very next few days to the closing, and where appropriate, the eviction of the said businesses. So, to speak, by decree n ° 52 of October 1, 2019, Edgard Anicet Mboumbou Miyakou had ordered the closure of drinking establishments installed near schools throughout the national territory.

and lives. Having a capitalistic spirit, they are mostly interested in making considerable financial benefits. For instance, in 2018, Antoine Relaxe (*Gabonactu*) informed: *"Selon les forces de police nationale, les mineurs sont de plus en plus présents dans les débits de boissons et parfois pendant les heures de cours et en uniforme."*[8] His statement joins our standing point on the phenomenon.

Bar tenders contribute to obliterating the government's regulatory policies aimed at protecting the pupils. They afford to break governmental laws and endanger the Gabonese youth just for the sake of egoistical financial motives. Those mercenaries encourage pupils to drink alcohol and to become negligent with their studies. Their cupidity puts Gabonese pupils' schooling dramatically in peril.

III.2.3. Alcohol Advertisement Near Schools

A survey by the World Health Organization[9] (WHO) in 2017 revealed that Gabon is the African country wherein alcoholic drinks are most consumed with an average of 9.01 litres per over-15-year-old consumer in a year. *Voxpopuli241* (2019) relates :

> *Dans un récent rapport de l'Organisation mondiale de la santé (OMS), il a été établi qu'un gabonais âgé de plus de 15 ans consomme en moyenne 9,01 litres de boissons alcoolisées par an, rapporte "Lasource". Une statistique peu glorieuse pour un pays qui aspire à l'émergence d'ici cinq années. C'est à se demander que font les autorités pour mettre un frein à cette dangereuse tendance.*[10]

According to such statistical data, it can be understood that Gabonese people drink alcohol not only precociously but also abusively. These empirical data thus reveal that Gabonese adolescents, especially pupils, are included in that drinking population. This means that Gabonese pupils are affected by the industry of alcohol production and consumption in Gabon.

A hugely powerful tool in prompting pupils to drink alcohol is an advertisement. As a matter of fact, when one makes a trip around Libreville, one will notice that

---

[8] According to the national police force, minors are increasingly present in drinking establishments and sometimes during school hours, wearing school uniforms.

[9] Founded in 1948, the WHO is the United Nations agency that connects nations, partners and people to promote health, keep the world safe and serve the vulnerable – so everyone, everywhere can attain the highest level of health. The WHO leads global efforts to expand universal health coverage. We direct and coordinate the world's response to health emergencies.

[10] In a recent report by the World Health Organization (WHO), it was established that a Gabonese over the age of 15 consumes an average of 9.01 litres of alcoholic beverages per year, reports 'Lasource'. An inglorious statistic for a country that aspires to emergence within five years. It makes one wonder what is being done by the authorities to put a stop to this dangerous trend.

advertisement contributes to encourage the consumption of alcohol at minors and pupils'. For example, some giant billboards near secondary schools such as Paul INDJENDJE GOUNDJOUT and Nelson MENDELA High Schools, advertise on behalf of famous beer and wine brands such as Régab, Beaufort, Castel, 33 Export, Vino Cola, and Booster, to name a few. *Voxpopuli241* (2019) describes:

> *Si vous vous rendez aux abords des établissements comme le lycée Paul INDJENDJET GONDJOUT, Nelson MANDELA, et même l'université Omar BONGO, votre vue est littéralement asphyxiée par l'exhibition des produits alcoolisés sur des panneaux publicitaires géants. De la promotion de la marque Beaufort, Castel, Booster ou Vino cola, on a en plein la vue ! Et dire que sont des futurs dirigeants qui sont formés dans cet environnement malsain. L'on peut dès lors pointer du doigt aux agents publics qui laissent prospérer cette insidieuse propagande de l'industrie de l'alcool.*[11]

Indeed, the aim of the advertisement is mainly to impact the subconscious of the beholders, to seduce and make them become potential customers of the advertised product. It uses catchy words and pretty pictures to make the advertised products look attractive to beholders. Thus, the giant billboards near secondary schools tremendously impact the subconscious of pupils and prompt them to go and consume these alcoholic drinks in the nearest drinking bars to their schools.

Fortunately, the government and some nongovernmental organisations somehow ensure to avoid pupils undergoing the dangers inherent to alcohol consumption and spare the latter from undergoing punishment such as definitive exclusions through some non-coercive educational processes. Their logic is that if pupils do not drink alcohol, they will not enter schools in a drunken mood, thus they will not be excluded from school.

III.3. Governmental and Nongovernmental Action against Alcohol Intake at Pupils'

The present section is dedicated to the presentation (and assessment) of governmental and nongovernmental entities as regards the phenomenon of alcohol intake at pupils'. One is expected to be presented some decrees and ordinances aimed to ward off underage alcohol consumption.

---

[11] If you go near secondary schools such as the Paul INDJENDJET GONDJOUT high school, Nelson MANDELA High School, and even Omar BONGO University, your sight is literally asphyxiated by the display of alcoholic products on giant billboards. We are in full view of the promotion of Beaufort, Castel, Booster or Vino cola. Heartbreakingly, future leaders are trained in this unhealthy environment. We can therefore point the finger at the public officials who allow this insidious propaganda of the alcohol industry to flourish.

III.3.1. Government Policymaking to Protect Pupils from Alcohol Intake

In Gabon policymaking by the executive power is also destined to protect minor people, including pupils, from the damages of alcohol intake. Since the early years of the independence of the country, the Gabonese government has been making some decrees intended to protect the minor people of its population from all sorts of abuse. These decrees or ordinances have been issued by either the President of the Republic or the whole government, through the council of ministers. In these decrees and ordinances, the government intends to keep the Gabonese pupils far from alcohol intake and alcohol selling businesses such as drinking bars, dancing bars, and nightclubs… Among these decrees and ordinances are three of them, particularly associated with protecting the minors from all abuse, setting conditions to start and manage an alcohol-selling business, and setting regulations for bars to be in accordance with the law and keep minors (including pupils) far from alcohol intake. These Decrees and Ordinances are presented as follows:

- Decree No. 00864/PR/MI/MD/CI of July 30, 1970, on drinking establishment regulation in the Gabonese Republic. As far as minors are concerned, the aim of this presidential decree is to forbid all people under eighteen years old (18) from buying and consuming alcoholic drinks. It also forbids the latter to be admitted into any alcohol selling structure. This decree aims to promote good behaviour at minors and spare them to be harmed by the diverse dangers of profligacy and alcohol intake.
- Ordinance No. 59/76 of 1 October 1976, on the protection of minors. The aim of this ordinance is to protect minors from all types of extrinsic and intrinsic abuse such as physical exploitation by adults and even alcohol intake by minors themselves. Thus, this ordinance aims to protect minors from any abuse from adults or from their own selves.
- Decree No. 0408/PR/MISPID of 26 December 2012 setting the conditions for the opening and operation of drinking establishments. As far as the safe schooling of Gabonese pupils is concerned, this decree intends to keep drinking establishments such as bars and clubs far away from public and private schools. This decree recommends keeping a minimal distance of two hundred metres (200 m) from every school in Gabon, so as to prevent pupils from drinking alcohol or from being harmed by some drunken alcoholic people near the school.
- Ministerial Decree No. 052 issued on 1 October 2019, through which the government announced the imminent closure of all drinking establishments located near (less than 200 m) primary, secondary and high schools across the

country. That decision aimed to reduce the acts of violence perpetrated by pupils while in an inebriated mood.

These four Decrees and Ordinances from the Gabonese government can be regarded as preventive steps to keep minors (including pupils) far from alcohol intake. The strictest enforcement of these decisions could considerably contribute to dissuading bar tenders from seeing minors and pupils as their clients. The enforcement of such decrees would also keep bars far from schools, and this will considerably reduce, or even put an end to the consumption of alcohol by pupils. Therefore, the strict enforcement of the above decrees would help ensure a considerable reduction of the rate of school dropouts due to alcohol intake in Gabon.

The Gabonese government considers alcohol intake by pupils as a serious problem. That is why they issued the above ordinance and decrees so that they serve as guidelines to prevent pupils from enduring the damages inherent to precocious alcohol intake. Thus, they practically ensure the effectiveness of these decisions through the contribution of the National Police Forces (NPF) whose mission is to make bar tenders and pupils to respect the law. Such was the case in October 2019, when the Ministry of Domestic Affairs utilised the NPF in order to definitively close all bars located less than two hundred metres (200 m) from schools. These bars were not in accordance with the Decree No. 0408/PR/MISPID of 26 September 2012. As a response, the Minister of Domestic Affairs decided to issue a ministerial order to resolve that problem. Alix Musavu (*GabonReview*, 2019) discloses :

> *Dans un communiqué rendu public ce 4 novembre, le ministère de l'Intérieur informe l'opinion et particulièrement les tenanciers des débits de boissons situés aux abords des établissements scolaires que «les Forces de police nationale procèderont dans les tout prochains jours, à la fermeture, et le cas échéant, au déguerpissement desdits commerces». Pour ainsi dire, par arrêté n°52 du 1er octobre 2019, Edgard Anicet Mboumbou Miyakou avait ordonné la fermeture des débits de boissons installés aux bords des établissements scolaires sur l'ensemble du territoire national.*[12]

The above statement explicitly certifies that the Gabonese government is deeply committed to protecting pupils from alcohol intake. Though somehow considerable, their efforts are not enough to eradicate the phenomenon. There still are bars near schools, and pupils go on entering these bars illegally. Indeed, three years after Ministerial Decree No 052 of 1 October 2019 was issued, that situation remains

---

[12] In a press release made public on November 4, the Ministry of the Interior informs the public and particularly the owners of drinking establishments located near schools that 'the National Police Forces will proceed in the very next few days to close, and where appropriate, the eviction of the said businesses'. So, to speak, by decree n ° 52 of October 1, 2019, Edgard Anicet Mboumbou Miyakou had ordered the closure of drinking establishments installed near schools throughout the national territory.

unchanged and visibly continues to plague the schooling of numerous pupils in Gabon. Concordantly, Lyonnel Mbeng Essone (2022) deplorably notes : *"Ces apprenants intègrent très tôt la possibilité de fréquenter les ces espaces [débits de boissons] réservés aux adultes. On continue de voir les élèves en uniforme dans les bars. Vous voyez un groupe [d'élèves] avec la même couleur de pantalon, ils enlèvent juste le haut pour qu'on pense qu'ils sont en civil"*[13] (*Gabon Media Time*). Unfortunately, the government cannot accomplish such a landmark task with policymaking alone. It needs helping hands. It needs to be assisted by governmental organisations (GOs), nongovernmental organisations (NGOs), teachers, and parents to remedy the rampant problem of alcohol intake by Gabonese pupils.

III.3.2. Anti-Alcohol Sensitisation Campaigns in Gabonese Schools

Sensitisation campaigns are included among the steps to fight against the alcohol consumption by pupils in Gabon. These campaigns are initiated by either governmental organisations or nongovernmental organisations. Such campaigns are undertaken in public and private schools with pupils as the main targets to be sensitised. The main aim of these sensitisation activities is to give pupils as much information about the various dangers inherent to alcohol intake as possible, to ensure their safe and successful schooling.

When it comes to sensitisation against alcohol, the commitment of three important governmental and nongovernmental entities deserves explicit acknowledgement. These are : *La Direction Générale des Œuvres Scolaires* (DGOS)[14], *l'Office Central de la Lutte Anti-Drogue (OCLAD)*[15], and *Agir pour le Gabon*[16]. They are well known for taking action to sensitise the population in general and pupils in particular.

In a 2018 interview, Mr Alexis Biyogo, Director of socio-educative activities at the Ministry of Education, claimed: *"Avec les élèves, nous travaillons sur les IST et VIH/Sida, la consommation des drogues et d'alcool [...] tous des problèmes très*

---

[13] These pupils integrate very early the possibility of frequenting these drinking places [drinking bars] allowed solely to adult people. We can still see pupils dressed in school uniforms drinking in bars. You may very often see a group of pupils with the same colour of trousers, but they just take their shirts off to look as dressed in civilian attire.

[14] *La Direction Générale des Oeuvres Scolaires*: It is a body of the ministry of national education whose role is to ensure the proper functioning of school life in primary and secondary schools in Gabon. This government body is also in charge of raising awareness of pupils on social matters in Gabon. It is the guarantor of good morals of pupils in Gabonese schools.

[15] L'OCLAD: Office Central de Lutte Anti-Drogue (Central Office for Anti-Drugs Fight). It is a section of the Gabonese national police whose mission is to fight against drug trafficking and consumption. However, this office also conducts awareness-raising activities against alcohol and drug consumption in secondary schools in Gabon.

[16] '*Agir pour le Gabon*' is a non-governmental organisation created in 1995 by Doctor Alphonse LOUMA. For 26 years, this NGO has been carrying out actions aimed to sensitise the Gabonese population to the dangers of alcohol, tobacco and drugs. The hobbyhorse of this NGO is sensitisation against drugs. Regarding students, this NGO conducts sensitisation campaigns in schools in Gabon to inform Gabonese youth about the dangers of alcohol and drugs.

courants, au cours de ces dernières années, dans les établissements scolaires. Nous avons élaboré des supports de communication sur les maux qui minent le milieu scolaire [...]"[17] (*L'Union*, 2018). The statement of Mr Biyogo presents the *DGOS* as a governmental bureau that conducts sensitisation campaigns to prevent such ills as HIV/Aids, drug, and alcohol abuse from undermining the studies of Gabonese learners.

In 2011, the *OCLAD* sensitised third form (4ᵉ) Gabonese learners of Collège Bessieux to the dangerousness of alcohol and drugs. The *OCLAD* targeted first cycle learners because of their young age and vulnerability to the dangers of alcohol and drugs. *ExcelAfrica* imparts: *"Les méfaits de la drogue, de l'alcool et des relations sexuelles précoces en milieu scolaire étaient donc au centre de cette séance d'échanges fructueux que le directeur général par intérim de l'Oclad a eus avec plus de 250 élèves, essentiellement inscrits dans les classes de 4e au collège catholique Bessieux"*[18] (2011, p. 1). The aim of that campaign was to deter pupils from consuming alcohol and tobacco, to avoid them enduring the social, health, and academic side effects due to the consumption of these substances. It was also aimed at entrusting these attendees with a mission to sensitise their peers to the dangerousness of alcohol and tobacco at school and home. *ExcelAfrica* adds: *" [...] il [Le Lieutenant-Colonel Major de Police, Victor Mounanga A'Mateba] les a exhortés [les élèves] à se constituer en messagers qui répandront à travers leur collège, la parole qui sauve: évitons le tabac, évitons l'alcool !"*[19] (p. 2).

Equally significant, in 2019, *Agir pour le Gabon* NGO conducted a sensitisation campaign against alcohol in many schools in the city of Libreville. The NGO took advantage of the twenty-first (21ˢᵗ) edition of the National Day without tobacco and alcohol to sensitise some pupils to the dangerousness of alcohol. *L'Union* (2018, p. 2) recounts the sensitisation campaign in the following manner:

> *Les enfants, très réceptifs aux messages des membres de l'ONG, ont été informés sur les dangers de l'alcool et du tabac. Ils ont été invités à être les porte-parole d'Agir pour le Gabon auprès de leurs parents afin que ces derniers prennent conscience des dangers auxquels ils les exposent en les envoyant acheter de l'alcool ou de cigarettes (...) Cette journée a été aussi l'occasion pour l'ONG d'interpeller une fois de plus les pouvoirs publics sur*

---

[17] With the students, we work on STIs and HIV/AIDS, the consumption of drugs and alcohol ... all very common problems in recent years in schools. We have developed communication materials on the evils that undermine the school environment.
[18] The harmful effects of drugs, alcohol and early sexual relations in schools were therefore at the centre of this session of fruitful exchanges that the acting director general of Oclad had with more than 250 students, mainly enrolled in 4th grade classes at the Bessieux Catholic Secondary School.
[19] [...] he [Lieutenant-Colonel major of police, Victor Mounanga A'Mateba] urged them [the pupils] to constitute themselves as messengers who will spread through their college, the word that saves: 'avoid tobacco, avoid alcohol'.

> *la non-application de la loi antitabac et de toutes les mesures prises pour juguler l'alcoolisme dans notre pays.*[20]

That news from *L'Union* not only gives the content of that sensitisation campaign to the dangerousness of alcohol, conducted by the NGO *Agir pour le Gabon*, but also indicates that the Gabonese government does not strictly enforce the laws passed with intent to curb alcohol consumption in Gabon.

The non-enforcement of the law means that, in Gabon, despite the law forbids minors (pupils) from drinking alcohol and forbids the latter from entering bars, these instructions are not really respected by both pupils and bar tenders. That situation proves that governmental decrees have a somehow insignificant impact on the fight against the consumption of alcohol at pupils' to some extent. Therefore, despite government decision-making to solve the matter of alcohol consumption by pupils, we notice that the situation does not improve. Pupils still drink alcohol while wearing school uniforms. They still enter bars despite being forbidden from doing so. They are still the victims of the profligacy linked to alcohol intake. They are still subject to the definitive exclusion due to alcohol intake at school. Thus, we think that the Decree No. 00864/PR/MI/MD/CI of July 30, 1970, on regulating drinking establishments in the Gabonese Republic should strictly be enforced.

Given that the government policymaking and NGOs' sensitisation activities against the alcohol intake by the minors tend to be somehow inefficient, it thus appears that the implication of teachers and parents is needed to continuously and insistently raise pupils' awareness on the dangerous of alcohol.

III.3.3. Teachers' and Parents' Implications in Anti-alcohol Sensitisation

The Gabonese Government is clearly a spearhead in the dynamic of protecting pupils from the myriad problems inherent to alcohol consumption. Its decrees, ordinances, and the intervention of the National Police Forces have a huge impact on the effectiveness of prevention against alcohol consumption by pupils. The same genuine commitment is noticed at GOs and NGOs. However, there are other actors involved in that ongoing struggle. These are teachers and parents, who are closer to pupils than the Government, GOs and NGOs can be. At first sight, teachers and parents share daily experiences with pupils. They are automatically regarded as the entities

---

[20] The children were very receptive to the messages from the members of the NGO. They were informed about the dangers of alcohol and tobacco. They were invited to be the spokespersons of *Agir pour le Gabon* with their parents so that the latter become aware of the dangers to which they expose them by sending them to buy alcohol or cigarettes… This day was also an opportunity for the NGO to once again challenge the public authorities on the non-application of the anti-smoking law and all the measures taken to curb alcoholism in our country.

who may sensitise pupils on a daily basis. Accordingly, they have a key role to play against alcohol consumption by pupils.

Teachers are immensely implicated in sensitisation in Gabon because they play a double role in the personal development of pupils. The role of teachers is associated with transmitting pedagogical knowledge and educational values to pupils. Thus, the role of teachers consists in both developing the intellectual competences of pupils and providing them with advice so that they could build their personality positively. In this sense, teachers can be regarded as external parents for pupils. This viewpoint is supported by blogger Yann Steph (*Overblog*, 2022) when he holds:

> Le rôle d'un enseignant transcende le fait de suivre un plan de cours et un horaire de travail spécifiques. Parce que les élèves et les enseignants passent autant de temps ensemble, l'enseignant devient par inadvertance un «parent externe». Donc, les enseignants peuvent être des mentors pour aider à mettre l'enfant sur la bonne voie. Dans ce rôle, l'enseignant peut encourager l'élève à être le meilleur possible, et aussi être une source d'inspiration et de conseils pour les élèves.[21]

As regards the above statement, it is clearly highlighted that teachers are as committed as parents in pupil's education. However, the dangerousness of alcohol is not much echoed by teachers. The latter mostly sensitise pupils on matters such as the dangerousness of tobacco, the harmfulness of hard drugs at pupils', unwanted pregnancies, sexually transmitted diseases, etc. It should be honestly admitted that sensitising pupils on such social and health matters is a very positive action, whereas teachers tend not to devote the same energy to deeply sensitising pupils on the dangerousness of alcohol, which unfortunately causes multiple social and health problems at pupils' as well.

As far as parents are concerned, they should instil good education to children. Therefore, they should dutifully straighten their children's conduct when the latter misbehave. Parents should contribute to sensitising their children to the dangerousness of alcohol as well. They might either use non-coercive or coercive methods to deter their children from drinking. Unfortunately, some parents seem latitudinarian with their children. That laxity from the parents does not help. It contributes to worsening the phenomenon, since their children do not restrict themselves to drinking solely at home.

---

[21] The role of a teacher goes beyond following a specific lesson plan and work schedule. Because students and teachers spend so much time together, the teacher inadvertently becomes an 'outside parent'. Thus, teachers can be mentors to help put the child on the right track. In this role, the teacher can encourage the student to be the best possible and be a source of inspiration and guidance for students.

They come to deepen and share their drinking experiences with their classmates at school.

Teachers' insignificant sensitisation and the laxity of parents over alcohol intake by children may have resulted from the fact that in Gabon, alcohol is considered as an inoffensive drug. Because the damage that alcohol intake can cause on the human organism is not immediate, people are more inclined to tolerate alcohol drinking by minors. For instance, a minor who smokes cigarettes or cannabis will be immediately scolded by society, whereas a minor who drinks alcohol will be tolerated and encouraged to drinking a bit more. From that standpoint, it should be borne in mind that alcohol is as dangerous as tobacco and cannabis in many respects. That is why we humbly think that *The Mayor of Casterbridge* can serve as an educational instrument for teachers to put much more stress on the dangerousness of alcohol. In other words, the educational articulations in that book can be of huge help to reveal the hampering effects of alcohol to our learners.

Chapter IV: Some Educational Articulations from the Novel to Raise Awareness on the Dangerousness of Alcohol Intake at Pupils'

This chapter is based on an analytic approach on the storyline of *The Mayor of Casterbridge*. This analytic approach helps show how the social content of Hardy's novel can be used for educational purpose, that is, to be exploited as an educational instrument to raise awareness on the dangerousness of alcohol intake at Gabonese pupils.

IV.1. Impelled by Drunkenness, Henchard Sells His Wife

In *The Mayor of Casterbridge*, the storyline opens with a job trip undertaken by Michael, Susan, and Elisabeth-Jane Henchard. The Henchard family migrates from a rural area to the town of Casterbridge, where Michael Henchard hopefully intends to find a job as a hay-trusser to feed his family. Exhausted by the lengthy trip, the family decides to halt at a country fair on the road to Casterbridge to rest and have breakfast before they pursue their trip as far as the town of Casterbridge.

Then, the family enters a furmity[22] booth to eat and have shelter for a short while. Later, shortly after they start to eat, Michael Henchard suddenly decides to order some rum to pour it into his basin of porridge and eat the mixture. The narrator reveals: *"He winked to her [the saleswoman] and passed up his basin in reply to her nod; when she took a bottle from under the table, slily measured out a quantity of its contents, and tipped the same into the man's furmity. The liquor poured in was rum. The man as slily sent back money in payment."* (Hardy, 1998, p. 9). As one may see, Henchard does not restrict himself to drinking solely one basin of rum. This first basin of liquor ends to drive him into an abusive consumption, which spontaneously starts to alter his personality. The text reads: *"At the fourth [basin of rum], the qualities signified by the shape of his face, the occasional clench of his mouth, and the fiery spark of his dark eye, began to tell in his conduct; he was overbearing—even brilliantly quarrelsome"* (Hardy, p. 10). This alteration of Henchard's personality due to the liquor is characterised by mind alteration: the loss of reason. The narrator evidences that alcohol is a mind-altering substance when Henchard is described as moving from being on a positive demeanour onto a negative one.

Because of alcohol, a man [as Henchard], who was previously devoted to finding a job to ensure the social wellbeing of his family has suddenly turned into a devilish

---

[22] According to the narrator, furmity is a kind of corn flour porridge mixed with raisins and milk.

person. Because of liquor abuse, Henchard comes to antagonise the idea of marriage and becomes orally invective to his wife. Overtly, he accuses her of being the main cause of his miserable economic and social situation. The narrator corroborates: *"I haven't more than fifteen shillings in the world, and yet I am a good experienced hand in my line. I'd challenge England to beat me in the fodder business; and if I were a free man again I'd be worth a thousand pounds before I'd done o't. But a fellow never knows these little things till all chance of acting upon 'em is pas."* (Hardy, p. 10). However, it should be ascertained that Henchard thinks he is poor because he does not have a good job but not because he is a married man. Unfortunately, alcohol has obliterated his sense of rationality and prompted him to see his wife as the source of his financial misery. Completely drunk, he thus undertakes to ditch the source of his misfortune. He sells his wife and baby daughter in an auction. Henchard clearly makes an offer to any eventual costumer: *"I'll sell her for five guineas to any man that will pay me the money and treat her well; and he shall have her for ever, and never hear aught o' me. But she shan't go for less. Now then—five guineas—and she's yours. Susan, you agree"* (Hardy, p. 13).

A sailor named Mr Newson agrees with buying Susan Henchard with her baby daughter, Elisabeth-Jane, for a five-guinea amount. After Henchard takes the money of this customer, he and his wife separate due to the bargain and Henchard's loss of reason. The narrator somehow symbolises divorce through Susan pulling off her wedding ring and leaving with her new husband [Mr Newson]: *"(...) she [Susan] took up the child and followed him as he made toward the door. On reaching it she turned, and pulling off her wedding ring flung it across the booth in the hay trusser's face. [...] Seizing the sailor's arm with her right hand, and mounting the little girl on her left, she went out of the tent sobbing bitterly"* (Hardy, p. 15). In short, alcohol has caused Henchard to make an irreversible and disgraceful deed by selling his wife. It appears that the narrator uses a serious narrative tone to appeal to readers' sensitivity and reveal the dangerousness of alcohol to the latter through the drunkenness of Michael Henchard and the dramatic consequences it entails in the storyline.

In the English classroom, these textual elements can help teachers as educational instruments to show them how alcohol can drive someone to lose their reason and commit harmful deeds that might hurt their nearest neighbourhood. The serious tone of such representations may contribute to dissuading pupils from drinking alcohol in Gabon.

IV.2. The Impactful Power of Abstinence: Henchard Becomes a Teetotaller[23] and Succeeds in Business

Alcohol can be considered as a key element in the novel. Though it is not a human-like character, alcohol plays a key role in the plot, that is, it appears as the most influential element as it comes to the analysis of the life of the Mayor of Casterbridge [Henchard], whose is rich in situation reversals such as moving from poverty to socio-economic uplift.

In the storyline, the narrative tells the reader that Henchard was prompted by alcohol when he sold his wife for a five-guinea amount to Newson. He clearly lost his mind when he did such a thing. The day after, Henchard regained sobriety characterised by serious remorse. The narrator depicts Henchard scolding himself and attempting to find his wife. Henchard claims: *""Yet she knows I am not in my senses when I do that!" he exclaimed. "Well, I must walk about till I find her [. . .] Seize her! Why didn't she know better, than bring me into this disgrace!"* (Hardy, p. 19). Ashamed for selling his wife, Henchard turned to his original conviction that he must somehow find his wife and his little Elizabeth-Jane, and put up with the shame as best he could. Despite a thoroughly but vain research, Michael Henchard gets outraged by the consequence of his unreasonable deed. Despite his willingness to repair his mistake, he realises that alcohol has caused him to lose his wife and baby daughter for good. Disappointed by the disgraceful sale of his beloved ones, Henchard decides to take a landmark oath against alcohol. He swears: *"I, Michael Henchard, on this morning of the sixteenth of September, do take an oath before God here in this solemn place that I will avoid all strong liquors for the space of twenty-one years to come, being a year for every year that I have lived. And this I swear upon the Book before me; and may I be strook dumb, blind, and helpless if I break this my oath."* (Hardy, p. 20). Henchard decides to become a teetaller for twenty-one years.

Later, that solemn oath from Michael Henchard is not without a consequence, since his economic and social situations considerably undergo some positive transformations. The narrator informs the readers that eighteen years later, Michael Henchard has become a rich businessman in the town of Casterbridge: *"They [Susan Newson and Elizabeth-Jane Newson] came in from the country, and the steaming horses had probably been travelling a great part of the night. To the shaft of each hung a little board on which was painted in white letters "Henchard, corn-factor and hay-*

---

[23] A teetotaller is a person who never drinks alcohol.

merchant." (Hardy, p. 60). The narrator reveals a considerable change in the economic situation of Micheal Henchard.

The formerly poor peasant hay-trusser is now evoked as a rich owner of a corn and hay factory. However, in the town of Casterbridge the mayoral position is granted to the richest man. Thus, Michael in dint of working hard Henchard has become the richest man and the Mayor of Casterbridge. We can notice Henchard's new social position when a passer-by informs Susan (the wife Henchard sold) about the new status of her former husband: *"If you mount the steps you can see 'em. That's Mr. Henchard the mayor at the end of the table, a facing ye; and that's the councilmen right and left Ah, lots of them, when they begun life, were no more than I be now!"* (Hardy, p. 33). Henchard has visibly experienced not only an economic uplift, but also a social uplift. Through such economic and social uplift, it appears that the narrator somehow intends to associate the social uplift of Henchard with his oath to quit drinking alcohol. Abstinence from alcohol seems to have provided Henchard with hard work as his new centre of interest. Therefore, Hardy is not far from leading us to consider abstinence from drinking alcohol as the main factor that fuelled Henchard's socio-economic uplift in the novel.

Considering Henchard's abstinence from drinking alcohol, which somehow contributed to turn him into a workaholic and successful man, we think that *The Mayor of Casterbridge* can be a vivid stimulus for Gabonese pupils who drink alcohol to quit it and become more focused on their studies.

IV.3. Inebriated, Henchard Ridicules Himself in Public

As regards everyday life in society, having a responsible behaviour is necessary for someone to be respected in their neighbourhood and to be entrusted with responsibilities. We should remind our Gabonese Pupils that well deportment is important not only to be respected, but also to succeed. Thus, we should remind them that alcohol intake can impel someone to behave improperly in public and ruin their reputation. Coming back to the novel, it is well worth saying that in *The Mayor of Casterbridge*, the narrator one more time associates the behavioural defects of Michael Henchard with alcohol intake.

In the storyline, the narrator announces that *"a royal personage was about to pass through the borough, on his course further west to inaugurate an immense engineering work out that way. He had consented to halt half-an-hour or so in the town, and to receive an address from the corporation of Casterbridge"* (Hardy, p. 262). To warmly welcome the royal personage into Casterbridge, The Town Council, headed by Donald Farfrae, the newly elected mayor who replaced bankrupt Henchard, meet on the Tuesday before the appointed day to arrange the details of the procedure.

Because he is no longer rich and mayor, The Council banishes Henchard and ejects him from the appointment. Therefore, Farfrea expels Henchard: *"I hardly see that it [Henchard's fake presence as an official] would be proper, Mr. Henchard,"* said he. *"The council are the council, and as ye are no longer one of the body there would be an irregularity in the proceeding. If ye were included, why not others?"* (Hardy, p. 263). Living his exclusion as a humiliation, Henchard decides to take his revenge on The Council. The narrator describes Henchard's anger and revengeful plan as such: *"I'll welcome his Royal Highness, or nobody shall!" he went about saying. "I am not going to be sat upon by Farfrae, or any of the rest of the paltry crew. You shall see."* (Hardy, p. 263). Henchard's revengeful plan is characterised by his desire to welcome the Monarch as an official even though he is no longer the mayor of Casterbridge.

In the morning of the appointed day, while the monarch is supposed to visit the town, the narrator informs that Henchard takes a day off and drinks rum: *"Henchard had determined to do no work that day. He primed himself in the morning with a glass of rum"* (Hardy, p. 264). He seems to be drinking rum that morning as a source of courage for him to achieve his revengeful disobedience to The Town Council. Later, the appointed time of the Monarch's visit comes. Unexpectedly, the rum that Henchard has been drinking for courage has mostly contributed to ridiculing him in front of the Monarch, the Council members, his relatives, and the crowd. As per the narrator, Henchard is 'staggering' while he is waving his New-jack flag to salute the monarch's cortege. The text reads: *"a man stepped before any one could prevent him. It was Henchard. He had unrolled his private flag, and removing his hat he staggered to the side of the slowing vehicle, waving the union-jack to and fro with his left hand, while he blandly held out his right to the illustrious personage"* (Hardy, p. 266). According to the *Collins Cobuild English Language Dictionary*, the verb *stagger* means *"to walk or move unsteadily, as if about to fall"* (p. 1417). The narrator uses the verb *stagger* to mean that Michael Henchard is immensely inebriated when he is saluting the Monarch. Not only is Henchard ridiculous for staggering publicly because he is drunk, but he is equally disrespectful to the Monarch whom he [Henchard] dares to salute in a drunk mood. Alcohol prompts him to both ridicule himself in public and disrespect the king. As a result, this misbehaviour contributes to ruin his reputation.

The ridiculous demeanour of Michael Henchard at this public ceremony impels people to scorn him so far. The narrator drives readers to understand that alcohol has prompted Henchard to misbehave in public, which gives Farfrea, the new mayor who used to be his employee, the opportunity to disrespect him: *"Farfrae with mayoral authority immediately rose to the occasion. He seized Henchard by the shoulder, dragged him back, and told him roughly to be off"* (Hardy, p. 267). Disrespectfully, Farfrea expels Henchard from the ceremony, as if he were a mere party-poorer[24]. This scornful demeanour of Farfrea upon his former employer and friend [Henchard] is rather a response to Henchard's misconduct in front of the Monarch. In this episode, Hardy depicts alcohol as a substance that may contribute to reducing a previously respected person [as Henchard, who was the respected mayor of Casterbridge] into a despised person in his neighbourhood. It can even contribute to ruining his/her reputation.

As regards this episode, teachers may use *The Mayor of Casterbridge* to highlight how much harmful alcohol can be to someone's behaviour and reputation. This public humiliation that Michael Henchard underwent might well serve as a striking argument to dissuade Gabonese learners from drinking alcohol. It might encourage them to be well behaved and respectful pupils.

---

[24] A party-poorer is a person who throws gloom over social enjoyment.

Chapter V: Some Proposed Activities to Implement *The Mayor of Casterbridge* in English Classes

The Acquisition of a language is noticeable in pupils who have acceptable handling of the four communicative skills. In order to achieve such performance, pupils should be involved in activities which favour the integration and development of the four skills. In that sense, the research paper proposes a set of activities whose aim is to help teachers develop the four communicative skills in their pupils. These activities include class debate, role-play, and dictation.

V.1. Role-play as an Interactive Activity to Raise Awareness on the Dangerousness of Alcohol Intake.

The *Collins Cobuild English Language Dictionary* (*Collins*, p. 1258) defines that *Role-playing* as *"the act of imitating the character and behaviour of a type of person who is very different from yourself, either deliberately, for example as a training exercise, or without knowing it"*. It can be applied to language teaching to get pupils more implicated in their learning and favour a student-centred acquisition of the target language. *The Mayor of Casterbridge* is rich in alcohol-linked articulations, so that the teacher can use it to create role-play to draw pupils' attention on the dangerousness of alcohol.

The role-play text script (appendix 4) adapted from the novel is based on the arrival of Michael, Susan and Elisabeth-Jane Henchard at the country fair near the town of Casterbridge (Hardy, pp. 5-20). In that episode the Henchard family enters a furmity booth to have breakfast. Then, Michael Henchard puts too much rum in his successively ordered basins of furmity[25] and gets drunken. It is under the influence of drunkenness upon himself that Michael Henchard sells his wife and baby daughter.

The English in this script has been kept as original as in the book's storyline to put pupils in contact with authentic English and immerse them in real-life situations of English practice. Firstly, the teacher should recommend that pupils consider the text *"Drunk, Henchard sells his wife for five guineas"* as a script in the role-playing phase. Secondly, the teacher randomly selects five (5) pupils out of the thirty-five pupils in the classroom, so that they perform in front of their classmates. He will necessarily select three boys and two girls according to the script. The three boys will respectively

---

[25] Furmity is a kind of porridge made of wheat flour and other ingredients boiled in water.

role-play Michael Henchard, the auctioneer, and Mr Richard Newson. The two girls will role-play Susan Henchard and the old saleswoman.

As regards the role-play performance, the teacher invites performers to step to the front. Before they start performing, the teacher takes 30 seconds to give instructions and clarify the fulfilment process. The activity consists in making the pupils acting out by reading from the script with strong emotions and gestures. The five actors respectively are supposed to embody the character they are assigned to role-play. During the performance the class should be quiet and attentive. This performing phase is planned to last five minutes at most.

In that activity, reading and role-playing were intentionally combined to integrate three skills in the same activity. In other words, such an activity is designed to develop reading, listening, and speaking in unison. The theme which was addressed in the script was intentionally selected to make pupils realise the dangerousness of alcohol.

V.2. Debate/Discussion on Henchard's Full Responsibility for his Wife's Sale

According to the *Collins Cobuild English Language Dictionary* (p. 363), a debate is *"a discussion about a subject on which people have different views"*. In terms of language teaching in the classroom, it refers to a formal contest in which the affirmative and negative sides of a topic are advocated by opposing groups.

The fulfilment of this activity requires the teacher to select a topic linked to alcohol from *The Mayor of Casterbridge*. This topic is formulated as follows: *"In the text, Michael Henchard sells his wife after he had drunk too much liquor. Do you think that Henchard is fully responsible for his action?"* the teacher writes on the board to ensure pupils good visibility and good understanding of the topic. For sake of good classroom management, the teacher can divide the classroom into three (3) groups of about 10 pupils. Then, he should explain the principle of the debate. Five (5) members in each group are going to defend the opinion that Henchard is fully responsible for his wife's sale, and the other five (5) members are going to oppose that opinion. The teacher lets each group of five (5) select a leader to organise group work.

Then, the teacher grants two (2) minutes to all groups for them to practise brainstorming and select their most relevant arguments. In the meantime, the teacher should move around the classroom to ensure that each pupil is implicated in the activity. Finally, as a moderator, he launches the debate by giving the floor to group 1.

As soon as group 1 has finished debating, group 2 takes the floor. Shortly after group 2, group 3 replaces them.

This activity is beneficial to improve speaking, writing, listening, reading skills and critical thinking. The activity is a golden opportunity for pupils to learn from one another about the dangerousness of alcohol intake. This activity should be allocated 10 minutes maximum.

V.3. Dictation to Improve Writing and Listening Skills at Pupils'

Dictation is the process of writing down what someone else has said. It provides a chance for pupils to model many writing behaviours such as handwriting, spelling, and sentence formation.

In this activity, the text (appendix 5) is selected from *The Mayor of Casterbridge*. A week before the dictation assignment, the teacher should distribute the text to pupils for them to memorise it at home and prepare the table assignment. During the fulfilment of the dictation assignment, the teacher reads the text twice while pupils are listening carefully to his readings. By the third reading, pupils write all the words the teacher pronounces on their respective assignment sheets till the end of the dictation assignment. The teacher should read slowly to allow all pupils to hear each word in all sentences he reads. This activity lasts eight minutes maximum. It is beneficial to develop pupils' writing, listening, and reading skills.

Conclusion of Part One

This part has helped to present *The Mayor of Casterbridge* as an authentic material to facilitate English language acquisition in a naturalistic environment of English use. It showed how teachers can use the novel to design some motivating activities destined to encourage the integrated development of the four communicative skills at pupils'. However, this part also revealed *The Mayor of Casterbridge* as a didactic instrument whose utility can go beyond its development of the functional aspects of English language. Indeed, the educational usefulness of the novel was proved by showing that the social content of it can be profitably exploited by teachers for educational purposes (such as raising pupils' awareness on the dangerousness of alcohol intake at pupils').

Part Two: Experimentation Phase

Introduction of Part Two

This part deals with the practical implementation of our research topic. To be clear, it presents the questionnaires and their results to assess (qualitatively and quantitatively) the relevance of our research work. Then, the practical implementation is made effective through two lesson plans. The part closes with some difficulties encountered and suggests some institutional solutions.

Chapter VI: Data Collection and Analysis

This chapter presents the procedure and instruments that have been necessary to conduct this research work, whose objective was to verify whether *The Mayor of Casterbridge* could help facilitate English language acquisition and raise awareness on the dangerousness of alcohol at Gabonese learners'.

VI.1. Data Collection

The data collection consists in presenting the research tools that have helped to gather the information needed and gauge the effectiveness of our didactic tool.

VI.1.1. Area of Study

The area of study refers to the place where the study was conducted. In fact, the research was carried out during the training period that lasted from February to May 2022 at Lycée National Léon MBA[26], also referred to as Complex Léon MBA[27]. This state high school is in the first district Northwest Libreville. The high school was founded in 1955. That 2021-2022 academic year, the head of the English Department was Mr Jean Bernard MAYISSA. The department comprised sixteen (16) teachers.

VI.1.2. Target Population

The research was conducted in the classrooms of 4e M14 (44 pupils) and 2nde S2 (35 pupils). The other population was made up of the teachers of English from Léon MBA compound. Eight (8) of them were involved in the study.

VI.1.3. Research Strategy

The data was based on both qualitative and quantitative methods, presented throughout two main questionnaires: the first one was addressed to pupils and the second one to teachers.

The *Oxford Online Dictionary of Business and Management* defines a questionnaire as *"a list of research or survey questions asked to respondents, and designed to extract specific information. It serves four basic purposes: to collect the appropriate data, to make data readable thanks to the analysis, minimize bias in formulating and asking questions and to make questions engaging and varied."* The questionnaire was selected among many others because we judged it as the easiest

---
[26] Léon MBA National High School is a State High school in Libreville, Gabon.
[27] Complex Léon MBA consists of Lycée Léon MBA, C.E.S Léon MBA 1, and C.E.S Léon MBA 2.

instrument to handle and the most effective process to gather needed information faster in the framework of this study.

VI.1.4. Data Collection Instruments

We opted to use two (2) questionnaires to conduct our inquiry and collect the data. As previously mentioned, one of the questionnaires is addressed to pupils and the other one is addressed to teachers. The questionnaire addressed to pupils was typed and presented in French, to facilitate their understanding of all questions and allow them to easily answer them. It was made of ten (10) questions intended to: a) get information about the different didactic materials and activities that have been involved in pupils' English language learning, b) inquire if pupils know much about alcohol intake, c) inquire if *The Mayor of Casterbridge* would be an enjoyable book for pupils to learn English. Then, the eleven questions (11) questionnaire addressed to teachers was written in a correct English. It is intended to: a) get information about the professional experience of each teacher, b) inquire if the activities used by the teachers are effective enough, c) inquire if the teachers usually use some British literature to teach English, d) get teachers' opinion on *The Mayor of Casterbridge* as an original didactic source to teach English.

VI.2. Results and Analysis

The following results came from the analysis of the questionnaires addressed to pupils and teachers. Firstly, the results from pupils' questionnaire will be presented. Secondly, it will be the turn of the answers from teachers' questionnaire to be revealed. Thirdly, the global assessment of the results will be given.

VI.2.1. Results from Pupils' Questionnaire

The questionnaire was addressed to forty-four (44), third form (4e M_{14}) pupils and thirty-five (35) fifth form (2nde S_2) pupils officially registered at Lycée National Léon MBA. All the seventy-nine (79) pupils who received the questionnaire designed for them regularly attend classes. Thus, the results compiled here are based on the answers provided by these seventy-nine pupils. The questionnaire is made of ten (10) questions, and some are multiple-choice questions. The results given result from the analysis of answers from question one (1) to question ten (10). The results are expressed in figures as numbers and percentages and are thoroughly interpreted.

Table 1 : *Question 1: vous apprenez l'anglais depuis…?*[28]

Duration / Class Names	3 years	4 years	5 years	6 years	7 years	Totals
4ᵉ M$_{14}$	39	4	1	0	0	44
2nde S$_2$	0	0	29	5	1	35
Pourcentages	88.7	9.1	2.2 / 82.9	14.3	2.8	79

This question was asked with intent to inform readers on how long the interrogated pupils have been learning the English language. After a thorough analysis of the data, we discovered that the majority (88.7%) of third-form pupils we interrogated have spent at least 3 years of English learning. While the most of fifth-form pupils (82.9%) that we interrogated have spent at least 5 years of English learning. We also noticed that more than 9% of the third form interrogated pupils have been learning for at least 4 years and that 2.2% of these pupils have spent at least 5 years of learning English. The results equally informed us that 14.3% and 2.8% of the interrogated fifth-form pupils have respectively spent more than 5 years of English learning. These results corroborate the fact that English learning is a process that requires at least six years in Gabonese secondary schools. English language acquisition as a lengthy process requires much time to occur. These figures reveal that English language acquisition at Gabonese pupils' is somehow hindered as regards the reduced time (110 min) now allocated to the English class per week in Gabonese schools. If English classes are allocated little time, teachers will hardly reach their teaching objectives.

Table 2: *Question 2: quel est votre niveau en anglais ?*[29]

Pupils' English levels	4ᵉ M$_{14}$	Percentage	2nde S$_2$	Percentage
No mastery of all four skills	35	79.6	20	57.2
Intermediate level	6	13.6	11	31.3
Advanced level	3	6.8	4	11.5
Total	44	100	35	100

The question was worth asking in the context of this study. It gives information on the level of our learners. Seventy-nine percent (35) of the third form pupils answered that they mastered none of the four communicative skills, whereas 13.6 % (6) of them said to be intermediate leaners and the other 6.8 (3) said to be advanced learners. We also discovered that 57.2 % (20) of the interrogated fifth-form pupils said master

---

[28] Table 1: Question 1: You have been learning English since…?
[29] Table 2: Question 2: What is your level in English?

neither of the four communicated skills, whereas 31.3 % (11) identified as intermediate and the other 11.5% identified as advanced learners. These advanced learners are suspected to be helped by their involvement in extra-class activities such as English clubs. However, the figures related those learners who are dramatically weak at English reveal that innovative techniques and material should be brought to make English language acquisition more effective in Gabon.

Table 3: *Question 3: avez-vous déjà fait des jeux de rôle pendant le cours d'anglais ?*[30]

Answers \ Classes	$4^e M_{14}$	Percentage	$2n^{de} S_2$	Percentage
No	38	86.3	29	82.8
Yes	6	13.7	6	17.2
Total	44	100	35	100

Teaching activities are at stake in that question. The aim of that question is to verify if learners are involved in activities that favour student centredness and interaction, since pupils tend to learn quicker for themselves and from their peers. Such activities may help to make pupils learn in a vivid atmosphere, which may motivate them to learn English. 86.3% percent of the interrogated third form and 82.8% of the interrogated fifth-form pupils answered "No", whereas 13.7% of the third form and 17.2% of the fifth form interrogated pupils answered, "Yes". As regards these figures, the practice of role-play remains highly unfashionable in English classes in Gabon. Teachers should use more activities to gradually increase the motivation of Gabonese learners to learn English.

Table 4: *Question 4: avez-vous déjà fait des débats pendant le cours d'anglais?*[31]

Answers \ Classes	$4^e M_{14}$	Percentage	$2n^{de} S_2$	Percentage
Yes	15	34	16	45
No	29	66	19	55
Total	44	100	35	100

The results from that question show that many pupils have seldom been involved in a debate or discussion during English classes. We observed that 34% of third-form pupils and 45% of fifth-form pupils acknowledged to already have been involved in

---

[30] Table 3: Question 3: Have you ever roleplayed during the English class?
[31] Table 4: Question 4: Have you ever had debates during the English class

class debate/discussion, whereas 66% of third-form pupils and 55% of fifth-form pupils acknowledge to never have been involved in such activities. The debate/discussion is both an interactive and motivational activity. It is a keen instrument toward language acquisition through intensive communication situations in the classroom. It may allow for an integrated and correlative improvement between listening and speaking skills at pupils'.

Table 5: *Question 5: quels sont les thèmes les plus évoqués par le professeur d'anglais ?*[32]

Cumulated answers from all Pupils / Themes	Frequency			
	Seldom	Very often	Most often	percentage
Teenage pregnancies and STDs	0		40	51
Juvenile delinquency	0	25		32
Drugs	14			17
Total	14 /79	25/79	40/79	100

Teenage pregnancies and STDs[33] (51%) and juvenile delinquency (32%) were the most apparent answers in that question. However, drugs encompassed 17% of the answers. Visibly, it appears from the above results that teachers are already committed in value transmission to pupils. These results also raise a fact: the dangerousness of drugs is not much echoed at school. *The Mayor of Casterbridge* could serve as a complementary didactic tool to raise pupils' awareness on the dangerousness of drugs, especially alcohol, as regards the behaviour of Michael Henchard, the protagonist of the novel. In learning from Henchard mistakes linked to alcohol abuse, pupils will apprehend how harmful alcohol intake can be to their safety and studies.

Table 6: *Question 6: quels sont les supports didactiques les plus utilisés par le professeur d'anglais ?*[34]

Cumulated answers from all Pupils / Didactic supports	Frequency			
	Never	Seldom	Most often	percentage
Texts	0		60	76

---
[32] Table 5: Question 5: What are the themes most mentioned by the teacher of English?
[33] STDs means Sexually Transmitted Diseases.
[34] Table 6: Question 6: What are the most common teaching materials used by the teacher of English?

Videos	0	9		11.4
Audios	0	10		12.6
Total	0	19/79	60/79	100

Texts recorded 76% of the answers, video 11.4%, and audios encompassed 12.6 % of the answers. It appears that the text is the most fashionable didactic instrument used for English language acquisition in Gabon. However, teachers could include videos and audios as motivational teaching supports, since pupils tend to show a keen motivation in learning English when new technology is involved in this process.

Table 7: *Question 7: aimez-vous les histoires qui se terminent par une leçon de morale ? Justifiez votre réponse.*[35]

Possible answers \ Most recurrent answers	Because such stories arouse sadness	Because such stories contribute to personal education
Yes	0	71/79
No	8/79	0
Percentage	10	90

The results of that question revealed that learners are attracted by stories that end with a moral lesson. Almost 90% of the pupils acknowledged to like stories with a moral lesson at the end, because they can help for personal education. However, a minority of them (10%) acknowledged to dislike such stories, because they often arouse a sad emotion in them. These figures reveal that teachers should use more of such stories with a moral lesson to both motivate and contribute to pupils' personal education.

Table 8: *Question 8: avez-vous déjà bu de l'alcool ?*[36]

Answers \ Classes	4ᵉ M$_{14}$	2ⁿᵈᵉ S$_2$		Percentage
Yes	8	15	23	29.2
No	36	20	56	70.8
Total	44	35	79	100

That question was asked to verify if secondary-school pupils often drink alcohol in Gabon. 29.2 percent of the interrogated pupils acknowledged to have drunk alcohol

---

[35] Table 7: Question 7: Do you like stories that end with a moral lesson? Justify your answer.
[36] Table 8: Question 8: Have you ever drunk alcohol?

already, whereas 70.8 % of the pupils claimed they had never drunk alcohol. Though most of these pupils do not drink alcohol, the minority who drinks helps reveal that drinking alcohol is part of pupils' habits in their schooling. These pupils who drink alcohol expose themselves and their schoolmates to be hurt by the myriad dangers inherent to underage alcohol intake. Teachers could use the social contents of *The Mayor of Casterbridge* as a vivid stimulus to make pupils who drink alcohol quit it to focus on their studies.

Table 9: *Question 9: est-ce que boire de l'alcool est une bonne chose ?*[37]

Most recurrent answers / Possible answers	Because it makes people feel happy in parties	Because it makes people Behave improperly	Because it may Cause health problems	Unable to justify their answers
No	0	10/79	10/79	56/79
Yes	3/79			
Percentage	3.7	12.6	12.6	70.8

The aim of that question was to get pupils to give their opinion on alcohol. 3.4% of the pupils thought alcohol drinking to be a good thing because it makes people feel happy in family parties.12.6 % of pupils considered alcohol drinking as a bad thing because it makes people behave improperly at home and in public. Another 12.6 % of the pupils said alcohol drinking is a bad thing because it may cause health problems, whereas almost 70.8% of the pupils thought alcohol drinking to be a bad thing, but they were unfortunately unable to justify their answers. From the previous pupils, it appears that teachers should intensively and deeply inform pupils on the dangerousness of alcohol to protect them from the dangers inherent to the consumption of that substance. For instance, they might use *The Mayor of Casterbridge* in such a task. This book deeply shows how harmful alcohol drinking can be to people through the dramatic relation that inextricably connects Michael Henchard's fate with alcohol drinking. This book may be helpful to dissuade pupils from drinking alcohol.

Table 10: *Question 10: seriez-vous content d'apprendre l'anglais à travers The Mayor of Casterbridge ?*[38]

Classes / Answers	$4^e M_{14}$	$2n^{de} S_2$
Yes	44/44	35/35
No	0/44	0/35
Percentage	100	100

---

[37] Table 9: Question 9: Is alcohol drinking a good thing?
[38] Table 10: Question 10: Would you be happy to learn English through *The Mayor of Casterbridge*?

Before pupils answered that tenth question, we orally provided them with the plot of the novel, so that their sentiment about the novel would not be a biased one. Amazingly, 100% of the pupils said they would be happy to learn English from a novel with such an interesting yet dramatic plot. Such a result clearly proves that pupils were keen to give this novel a chance to be explored. It equally shows their keenness to know deeper about the dangerousness of alcohol and avoid being harmed by the consumption of such a mind-altering substance.

VI.2.2. Results from Teachers' Questionnaire

The following figures result from the analysis of the data collected from eight (8) teachers from Complex Léon Mba. The questionnaire addressed to teachers comprises eleven (11) correctly English-written questions. Some are multi-choice questions and others are multi-choice justifiable questions.

Table 11: *Question 1: What is your qualification?*

Qualifications	CAPES	CAPC	Bachelor's degree	Master's degree
Number	4	2	1	1
Percentage	50	25	12.5	12.5

This question provided qualitative data about the qualification of the interrogated teachers in our study. We noticed that teachers have respectively, 50% CAPES (teachers teaching from first form to upper sixth form), 25% CAPC (teachers teaching in secondary school), 12.5 % bachelor's degree (teachers with a faculty diploma, hired on service needs), 12.5% Master's degree (equally with a faculty diploma, hired on service needs). This inquiry was useful to identify the teachers who have received training at Ecole Normale Supérieure and have necessarily received didactic and pedagogic training. It equally helps identify the teachers who have just a faculty training and have never received the necessary didactic and pedagogic knowledge inherent to English language teaching.

Table 12: *Question 2: How long have you been teaching English?*

Teaching experience	10 years	5 years	1 year
Number	5	2	1
Percentage	62.5	25	12.5

That question was useful to know about the teaching experience of the audience. We learned from the results that out of eight (8) teachers, 62.5 % (5) have at least 10 years of experience, 25% (2) have at least 5 years of experience, 12.5% (1) has 1 year of experience (obviously a newly appointed teacher).

Table 13: *Question 3: Do you design clear objectives when you prepare your lesson?*

Objectives	Prominence of Thematic contents	Prominence of skill improvement	Combination of both aspects
Number	6	1	1
Percentage	75	12.5	12.5

As regards that question, we aimed to inquire whether teachers insist only on the functional aspects of language acquisition, or they target other aspects as theme-based contents. Accordingly, 75% of teachers said they employed thematic contents during lessons, 12.5% said that they gave a prominence to functional aspects, and 12.5% said they made a combination between both.

Table 14: *Question 4: What subjects do you teach to pupils?*

Subjects	Politics	Social	Economics	Entertainment	Other
Number	4	3	1	0	0
Percentage	50	37.5	12.5	0	0

Here, we aimed to emphasise the orientation of the thematic contents used by teachers. Three main areas were mostly evoked: Politics (50%), social (37.5%), and economics (12.5%). We think that social-based contents should be given more prominence in lessons. In a society where minors are vulnerable to scourges such as drugs and alcohol teachers should extensively use related social supports for value transmission and sensitisation.

Table 15: *Question 5: What type of support do you often use?*

Subjects	Texts	Videos	Audios	Other
Number	5	1	2	0
Percentage	62.5	12.5	25	0

Here, we aimed to confirm the text as the most employed support in Gabon. Unsurprisingly, the text came first out of the inquiry with 62.5%. Audios came second with 25%, and videos came last with 12.5% of answers. The pre-eminence of the text explains itself since some teachers do not master how to apply new technology in language teaching, so they do not venture to use it and restrict themselves to using texts. Another factor which explains that situation is that classrooms lack of facilities such as electricity and internet connection. That tendency should be reversed since the contribution of new technologies to English language acquisition has been proved in developed countries. We should integrate newer technologies to accelerate English language acquisition at Gabonese learners' to pragmatically enable an upcoming era of bilingualism for Gabon in the Commonwealth.

Table 16: *Question 6: What is the impact of your activities on pupils?*

Pupils' sentiments according to teachers	Motivated	Bored, tired, and lost
Number	7	1
	87.5	12.5

Almost 87.5 % of teachers answered that their pupils felt motivated when involved in activities. The reason for such a motivation derives from the ability of teachers of English to strive to involve pupils in engaging and interactive activities. These teachers aim to immerse Gabonese learners into naturalistic conditions of English use, to circumvent the difficulties inherent to the challenge of teaching/learning English in an E.F.L context. 12.5% of teachers asserted that their pupils felt either bored, tired, or lost during activities. They claimed that pupils were not attentive in afternoon classes. Perhaps it is due to tiredness and hunger, which are mostly apparent at that precise moment of the day.

Table 17: *Question 7: Have you ever used a literary content as a didactic support?*

Teachers' answer	Yes	No
Number	8	0
Percentage	100	00

The results showed that 100% of teachers acknowledged to have used literary texts in their classes. The aim of this question was to see if literary text were used in English classes. It confirms that Gabonese learners are accustomed to reading literary contents in English classes.

Table 18: *Question 8: From which literature are these literary contents taken?*

Literatures	African literature	British literature	American literature
Number	5	1	2
Percentage	62.5	12.5	25

The results confirmed that the African literature is the most used for English language acquisition in Gabon. Expectedly, 62.5% of teachers said they employed African literature in their classes, 25% of American literature, and 12.5 % of British literature. Teachers of English consider the African literature as the most immediate and reliable source for them to find social and educational inputs for the personal development of pupils, because the social realities depicted in African novels strongly resemble the social realities in Gabon. This situation tends to disinterest them in using other literature than the African one. The aim of that question was profoundly to show that the British literature is the least used for English language acquisition in Gabon. It is somehow paradoxical that English language comes from the United Kingdom, but the British literature is almost inexistent in the English language acquisition process in Gabon. This question aims to call for teachers to provide a more varied literary experience and open-mindedness through a balanced use of these three literatures.

Table 19: *Question 9: Have you ever read The Mayor of Casterbridge by Thomas Hardy?*

Those having read the book	Yes	No
Number	1	6
Percentage	12.5	87.5

As regards the results, a few teachers of English have ever read *The Mayor of Casterbridge* by Thomas Hardy. 87.5% of teachers acknowledged to have never read the novel, whereas only 12.5% of teachers said to have ever read it. Such data helped reveal *The Mayor of Casterbridge* as an original novel unknown to many teachers of English.

Table 20: *Question 10: Have you ever used The Mayor of Casterbridge as a didactic support?*

Those having used the book As a didactic support	Yes	No
Number	0	8
Percentage	0	100

Unsurprisingly, even if some of them have read *The Mayor of Casterbridge*, 100% of teachers confirmed to have never used this book in their classes. The aim of that question in our study is to propose *The Mayor of Casterbridge* as an authentic material for English language acquisition and raise awareness on the dangerousness of alcohol at pupils'. The rich linguistic and social contents of this book could help teachers of English to attain such objectives.

Table 21: *Question 11: Using The Mayor of Casterbridge to teach English would be? a) Interesting b) Boring c) Risky*

Answers	Justifications	Because it may make the British literature more fashionable for English language acquisition in Gabon	Because it may contribute to stop the proliferation of drug abuse at Gabonese learners'
Interesting		3	5
Boring			
Risky			
Percentage		37.5	62.5

Wonderfully, 37.5% of teachers thought *The Mayor of Casterbridge* would be an interesting book to help increase the use of the British literature for English language acquisition in Gabon. Considering the social contents of *The Mayor of Casterbridge*, 62.5% of teachers thought this novel to be an interesting educational material to stop the proliferation of drug and alcohol abuse by Gabonese learners. As a whole, 100% of these teachers are eager to give this book a try in their classes.

VI.2.3. Assessment

An overall observation on the previous results confirms that teachers of English are favourable to employing some British literature for English language acquisition through *The Mayor of Casterbridge* by Thomas Hardy. They view this book as an educational instrument to prevent pupils from being harmed by the numerous dangers inherent to underage alcohol intake. Therefore, these results indicate that the respondents think this novel might be the adequate instrument to develop the functional aspects for English language acquisition and raise awareness on the dangerousness of alcohol at pupils'. In short, these results tend to legitimise the implementation of *The Mayor of Casterbridge* for English language acquisition in Gabon.

Chapter VII: Experimental Lessons

This chapter proposes two experimental lessons, which were implemented in $4^{ème} M_{14}$ and 2nde S_2 at Lycée National Léon MBA. The chapter also highlights some strengths and weaknesses observed during the respective delivery of the two lessons.

VII.1. Lesson Plan 1

Text: Michael Henchard Becomes a Teetotaler[1].

Shortly after selling his wife and baby daughter because he was drunk, Michael Heanchard entered the church to take his oath. The hay-trusser deposited his basket by the font and walked up the nave till he reached the altar. He opened the gate to enter the sacrarium, where he seemed to feel a sense of the strangeness for a moment. Then, he knelt upon the foot-pace. Dropping his head upon the closed book which lay on the Communion table, he said aloud: I, Michael Henchard, on this morning of the sixteenth of September, do take an oath before God here in this solemn place that I will avoid all strong liquors for twenty-one years to come. And I swear this upon the Book before me. Therefore, if I break this oath, may I become a blind and miserable man forever. When he had said it and kissed the big book, Henchard arose, and felt happy to start a life in a new direction.

1. A person who abstains from drinking alcohol.

Adapted from *The Mayor of Casterbridge* by Thomas Hardy, pp. 19-20.

CLASS DETAILS

School year: 2021-2022

Date: Monday, 16 May 2022

School Name: Léon MBA National High School

Subject: English

Class level: $4^e M_{14}$ (third form)

Class size: 44

Duration: 55 min

Teacher trainee's names: MENDOME MBANZOGUE Augustin Orsini

Lesson title: Reading comprehension and revision of the simple past

Text title: "Michael Henchard Becomes a Teetotaller."

Skill focus: speaking, reading, writing

Teaching aids: Board, chalk, handouts, flipcharts

Rationale for the text: This excerpt has been chosen because we want to discuss the dangerousness of alcohol with pupils, and by the way encourage pupils who drink alcohol to quit it and focus on their studies.

OBJECTIVES

General Objectives

GO1: understanding a text on abstinence from alcohol.

GO2: reviewing the simple past

Specific Objectives:

By the end of the lesson, the learners should be able to:

SO1 of GO1: use new words

SO2 of GO1: answer question from the text

SO1 of GO2: identify the regular simple past

SO2 of GO2: put a verb in affirmative, negative, and interrogative simple past

SO2 of GO2: use the simple past in the right context

LESSON PROCEDURE

I-   PRE-READING ACTIVITIES

1. **Warm-up (3 min)**

NB: T= teacher / SS=Students

The teacher greets the class immediately he comes in

T to SS: Good morning class!

SS to T: Good morning, Sir!

T to SS: We are fine, thank you; and you?

T to SS: I am fine too. Thank you! Sit down class!

2. **Lead-in (3 min)**

The teacher tells a short story and asks the opinion of the pupils at the end.

The story goes this way: In 2018, two 4e students of Paul Marie Yembit high school of Ndéndé entered the school after drinking alcohol. They entered the classroom in an inebriated mood. Alcohol prompted these students to behave disrespectfully to their teachers. The behaviour of these students impelled the disciplinary counsel to exclude the two offending students definitively from the high school. In that story alcohol has been the main factor of the definitive exclusion of these students.

T to SS: Class do you think that alcohol is a good or a bad thing?

SS to T: It is a bad thing Sir!

T to SS: Great class! Today, we are going to see a text on abstinence from alcohol.

II-   WHILE READING ACTIVITIES

3. **Reading Aloud (4 min)**

The teacher reads the first paragraph of the text and points three pupils to continue the reading while telling them to underline difficult words to pronounce and get the meaning.

4. Vocabulary (7 min)

The teacher designs an activity on the vocabulary. He writes the difficult words of the text on the left and their meaning on the right. He then asks the students to match every difficult word with their corresponding meaning.

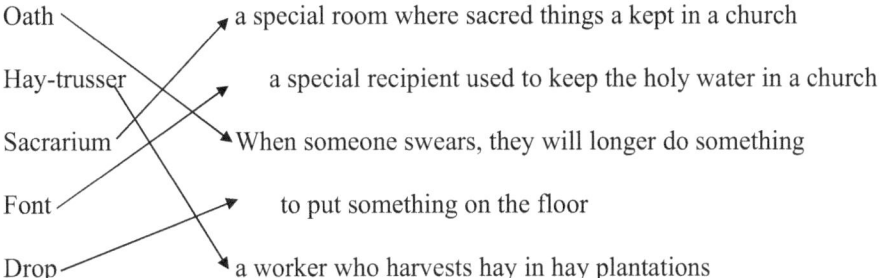

Oath — a special room where sacred things a kept in a church

Hay-trusser — a special recipient used to keep the holy water in a church

Sacrarium — When someone swears, they will longer do something

Font — to put something on the floor

Drop — a worker who harvests hay in hay plantations

5. Comprehension questions (13 min)

The teacher hands out a pair work (two by two) activity and gives instructions based on the task to do.

The activity goes as follows: Are the following statements True (T) or False (F)? Justify your answers by quoting from the text. Mention the lines.

	Statements	T	F	Justification	Line
A	Henchard swore to no Longer drink liquor for Twenty-one years	T		I, Micheal Henchard, take the oath… I will avoid all strong liquors for twenty-on years…	L5-7
B	Henchard sold only his wife Wife because he was drunk		fF	Shortly after selling his wife and baby daughter because he was drunk…	L1
C	Henchard is a hay-trusser	TT		The hay-trusser deposited his basket by the font…	L2
D	Hench took his oath to stop Drinking at the marketplace		FF	Michael Heanchard entered the church to take his oath.	L2

I- POST-READING ACTIVITIES

6. Grammar point (13 min)
The simple past

1) **Structure: regular verb**
   Verb + ED

E.g. open = open+ed= open**ed**; drop = drop+ed= dropp**ed**; carry= carry+ed= carr**ied**

2) Different forms

– Affirmative form: Subject +Verb + **ED**

E.g: Michael Henchard **opened** the door and **entered** the church, then he **dropped** his basket.

– Negative form: **Subject + did + not+ verb (infinitive)**

E.g: Michael Henchard **did not restrict** himself, he drank four basins of liquor.

– Interrogative form: **Did+ Subject + verb (infinitive) +?**

E.g: **Did** Michael Henchard **sell** his wife?

3) Use

The simple past is used to express past actions or events.

Activity: Use the Simple past to put the verb into the correct form.

1) Michael Henchard (to scold) himself for selling his wife and baby daughter (+)
   ……………………………………………………………………………………

2) Farfrea (to expel) Henchard from the ceremony because he was drunk (?)
   ……………………………………………………………………………………..

3) The population (to elect) Henchard as the Mayor of Casterbridge (-)
   ……………………………………………………………………………………

Expected answers: 1=scolded; 2=Did Farfrea expel; 3= The population did not elect Henchard…

7. Follow up activities (8 min)

Topic for group discussion (to be performed in class): the teacher puts pupils in groups of four and asks them to discuss, share ideas on the possible benefits that abstinence could bring into Henchard's fate.

Homework: Group dissertation

At home, in groups of three pupils write an eight-line essay in which you give some dangers linked to the consumption of alcohol: for next week.

Administration tasks.

- Attendance checking
- Logbook filling.

VII.2. Lesson Plan 2

Text: Drunk, Henchard Sells His Wife Susan for Five Guineas.

After eating his porridge mixed with some liquor, Michael Henchard chain drinks four basins of liquor. Suddenly, he goes drunk and starts to talk nastily to his wife [Susan] as well. He accuses her of being the source of his miserable financial condition. Shortly after, Michael decides to sell Susan with their baby daughter [Elisabeth-Jane] to a sailor [Mr Newson] in an auction for a five-guinea amount of money.

Henchard: I married at eighteen, like the fool that I was and this is the consequence of it. I haven't more than fifteen shillings in the world, and yet I am a good experienced hand in my line.

Henchard: For my part I don't see why men who have got wives, and don't want 'em, shouldn't get rid of 'em. Hey? Why, begad, I'd sell my wife this minute, if anybody would buy her!

Henchard: Well, then, now is your chance; I am open to an offer for this gem of creation.

Susan: Michael, you have talked this nonsense in public places before. A joke is a joke, but you may make it once too often, mind!

Henchard: I know I've said it before; I meant it. -All I want is a buyer. Will someone among you buy my goods?

Susan: Mike, Mike, this is getting serious. Oh—too serious!

Henchard: Will anybody buy her? Her present owner is not at all to her liking!

Henchard: Now, who's auctioneer?

Auctioneer: I am! Who'll make an offer for this lady? She's worth two guineas!

Saleswoman: Behave yourself moral, good man, for Heaven's love! Ah, what a cruelty is the poor soul married to!

Henchard: Set the price higher, auctioneer!

Auctioneer: Now, the lady is worth three guineas… four guineas.

Henchard: I'll sell her for five guineas to any man that will pay me the money and treat her well; and he shall have her for ever, and never hear aught of me.

Henchard: Do any body give it? - Yes or No?

Mr Newson: Yes, I do!

Henchard: Saying is one thing, and paying is another. Where's the money?

Susan: Before you go further Michael, listen to me. If you touch that money, I and this girl go with the man. Mind, it is a joke no longer.

Henchard: I take the money: the sailor takes you. That's plain enough. It has been done elsewhere and why not here!

Susan: Mike, I've lived with you a couple of years, and had nothing but temper. Now I'm no more to you; I'll try my luck elsewhere. It will be better for me and Elizabeth-Jane both. So, good-bye.

Adapted from *The Mayor of Casterbridge* by Thomas Hardy, pp. 5-20.

CLASS DETAILS

School year: 2021-2022

Date: Wednesday, 18 May 2022

School Name: Léon MBA National High School

Subject: English

Class level: 2nde S_2 (fifth form)

Class size: 35

Duration: 55 min

Teacher trainee's names: MENDOME MBANZOGUE Augustin Orsini

Lesson title: Reading comprehension and revision of the simple past

Text title: "Drunk, Henchard sells his wife for five guineas."

Skill focus: speaking, listening, and reading

Teaching aids: Board, chalk, handouts, flipcharts

Rationale for the text: This excerpt has been chosen because I want to discuss the dangerousness through a text that students can act out for them to realise that alcohol is a dangerous mind-altering substance which may prompt an inebriated person to harm people in his nearest neighbourhood.

OBJECTIVES

General Objectives

GO1: showing alcohol as a dangerous substance that may drive someone to act harmfully.

GO2: reviewing the imperative

Specific Objectives:

By the end of the lesson, the learners should be able to:

SO1 of GO1: use new words learned from the text

SO2 of GO1: answer questions from the text

SO1 of GO2: Identify the singular and the plural imperatives

SO2 of GO2: use the imperative to give orders, instructions, suggestions, and advice.

LESSON PROCEDURE

I- PRE-ROLE-playing ACTIVITIES

1. **Warm-up (3 min)**

NB: T= teacher / SS=Students

The teacher greets the class immediately he comes in

T to SS: Good morning class!

SS to T: Good morning, Sir!

T to SS: We are fine, thank you, and you?

T to SS: I am fine too. Thank you! Sit down class!

2. **Lead-in (5 min)**

To introduce the lesson the teacher will use a super large picture in which a drinking man is sleeping at a bar. The teacher will show the picture to attentive pupils. Then, he will ask them: *"class what you can see on this picture?"* The students are expected to answer: *"Sir, we can see a drunk sleeping man on that picture."* Then, the teacher will ask: *"what do you think about this drunk man? Is drinking alcohol a bad or a good thing?"* These questions about the drunk man expect pupils to see alcohol as a bad thing. Shortly after the students have somehow given such an answer, the teacher will say: *"Very good job class, now, today we are going to read and role-play on a text that deals with the dangerousness of alcohol"*.

Source: Google Chrome images accessed on July 10, 2022

II- WHILE ROLEPLAYING ACTIVITIES

3. Role-playing/reading (10 min)

This activity combines reading and role-play. The English in the text/script has been kept as original as in the novel to put pupils in contact with authentic English, and immerse them in real-life situations of English practice. First, the teacher distributes the text/script entitled "*Drunk, Henchard sells his wife for five guineas*" to all pupils. After distributing the text/script, the teacher randomly selects five (5) pupils out of the thirty-five pupils in the classroom, so that they perform in front of their classmates. Then, he selects three boys and two girls among pupils. According to the script, the three boys respectively roleplay Michael Henchard, the auctioneer, and Mr Newson. The two girls respectively roleplay Susan Henchard and the old saleswoman.

The fulfilment of that activity develops in two stages: the reading phase and the role-playing phase. As for the reading phase, it lasts three (3) minutes. The teacher reads the script loudly with emotions and gestures while the pupils are following his reading carefully. After reading, the teacher randomly points out five pupils to read the text loudly while their peers are following the reading in silence. The teacher should correct pronunciation mistakes during the reading of the text script by students during the reading session.

The role-play script (appendix 4) adapted from the novel is based on the arrival of Michael, Susan and Elisabeth-Jane Henchard at the country fair near the country town of Casterbridge (Hardy, pp. 5-20). In that episode the Henchard family enters a furmity booth to have breakfast. Then, Michael Henchard puts some too much rum in his successively ordered basins of furmity[39] and gets drunken. It is under the influence of drunkenness upon himself that Michael sells his wife and daughter.

The English in this script has been kept as original as in the book's storyline to put pupils in contact with authentic English, and immerse them in real-life situations of English practice. Firstly, the teacher recommends that pupils consider the text entitled '*Drunk, Henchard sells his wife for five guineas*' as a script during the role-playing phase. Secondly, the teacher randomly selects five (5) pupils out of the thirty-five pupils, so that they perform in front of their classmates. He exactly selects three boys and two girls according to the script's characters. The three boys are supposed to role-play characters Michael Henchard, the auctioneer, and Mr Newson. The girls respectively role-play characters Susan Henchard and the old saleswoman.

---

[39] Furmity is a kind of porridge made of wheat flour and other ingredients boiled in water.

As regards the role-play performance, the teacher invites performers to step to the front. Before they start performing, the teacher takes 30 seconds to give instructions. The activity consists in making the students acting out by reading from the script with strong emotions and gestures. The five actors respectively embody the character they are assigned to play. During the performance the class should be quiet and attentive. This performing phase is planned to last five minutes at most.

In that activity, reading and role-playing were intentionally combined to integrate three skills in the same activity. In other words, this activity is designed to develop reading, listening, and speaking in unison. The theme which was addressed in the script was intentionally selected to make pupils realise the dangerousness of alcohol consumption.

4. Vocabulary (5 min)

The teacher designs an activity on the vocabulary. He writes the difficult words of the text on the left and their shuffled synonyms on the right. He then asks pupils to match every difficult word with their synonyms. This activity aims to enrich pupils' vocabulary, provide them with an advanced-English lexicon to give them appropriate writing instruments for the baccalaureate English-written exam.

Match each word on the right with its corresponding synonym on the left:

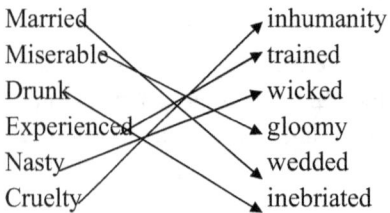

5. Comprehension questions

Tick the correct answer to each statement

1. At the furmity booth, Michael Henchard drank ... basins of liquor.

   o   One
   o   Six
   o   Four

2. When he became drank, Michael Henchard started to talk ... to his wife

- Kindly
- Nastily
- Tranquilly

3. Michael sold Susan for to Newson because he was…

- Wicked
- Disgusted by her
- Drunk

4. Michael sold Susan to Newson for a … amount of money.

- 50 dollars
- 1000 XFA
- 5 guineas

Expected answers: 1=four; 2=nastily, 3=Drunk; 4=5 guineas.

III- POST-ROLE-PLAYING ACTIVITIES

6. Grammar point (15 min)
The imperative

Use: the imperative is used to:

➢ Give some advice: **Behave yourself moral, good man**, for Heaven's love! (L19).
➢ Give command and order: **Set the price higher**, auctioneer! (L21).

Singular imperative:

– -Affirmative form: infinitive verb +!

  E.g: **Mind**, it is a joke no longer! (L28)

– Negative form: Do +not + infinitive verb. **NB: Do + not= Don't**
  E.g: **Don't set** the price high auctioneer!

Plural imperative:

– -Affirmative: Let +us + infinitive verb. **NB: Let +us= Let's.**

  E.g: **Let's set** the price high auctioneer!

- -Negative form: Let+ us + not + infinitive verb. **NB: Let + us + not = Let's not.**

E.g: **Let's not set** the price high auctioneer!

Activity: Match the two columns to give instructions:

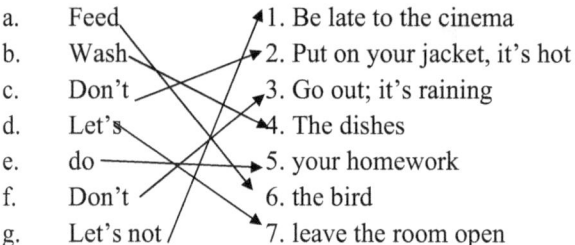

a. Feed
b. Wash
c. Don't
d. Let's
e. do
f. Don't
g. Let's not

1. Be late to the cinema
2. Put on your jacket, it's hot
3. Go out; it's raining
4. The dishes
5. your homework
6. the bird
7. leave the room open

Debate: (8 min)

The fulfilment of this activity requires the teacher to select a topic linked to alcohol from *The Mayor of Casterbridge*. This topic is formulated as follows: *'In the text, Michael Henchard sells his wife after he had drunk too much liquor. Do you think that Henchard is fully responsible for his action?'* the teacher writes on the board to ensure pupils a good visibility and good understanding of the topic. For sake of good classroom management, the teacher can divide the classroom into three (3) groups of about 10 pupils. Then, he should explain the principle of the debate. Five (5) members in each group are going to defend the opinion that Henchard is fully responsible for his wife's sale, and the other five (5) members are going to oppose that opinion. The teacher lets each group of five (5) select a leader to organise group work.

Then, the teacher grants two (2) minutes to all groups for them to practise brainstorming and select their most relevant arguments. In the meantime, the teacher should move around the classroom to ensure that each pupil is implicated in the activity. Finally, as a moderator, he launches the debate by giving the floor to group 1. As soon as group 1 has finished debating, group 2 takes the floor. Shortly after group 2, group 3 replaces them.

7. Follow-up

Homework: Prepared Dictation

Read carefully and memorise this text at home, a dictation assignment will be based on it. Prepare the dictation for next week.

Dictation: The Physical Portrait of Micheal Henchard.

Micheal Henchard was of a fine figure, swarthy, and stern in aspect; he showed in profile a facial angle so slightly inclined as to be almost perpendicular. He wore a short jacket of brown corduroy, newer than the remainder of his suit, which was a fustian waistcoat with white horn buttons, breeches of the same, tanned leggings, and a straw hat overlaid with black glazed canvas. At his back he carried by a looped strap a rush basket, from which protruded at one end the crutch of a hay knife, a wimble for hay-bonds being also visible in the aperture. His measured springless walk was the walk of the skilled countryman as distinct from the desultory shamble of the general labourer.

Adapted from *The Mayor of Casterbridge* by Thomas Hardy, p. 5.

Administration tasks

- Attendance checking
- Logbook filling.

VII.3. Strengths and Weaknesses of the Two Lessons

Obviously, the two experimental lessons we had with the learners had some strengths and weaknesses that we will present in the lines below.

VII.3.1. Strengths of the Lessons

The two lessons implemented presented some strengths. We can mention four of them as follows: opportunity to communicate exclusively in English, opportunity for integrated improvement of the four skills, horizontal and vertical interactions, pupils' motivation, and pupils' mutual education.

The first strength observed while implementing lesson 1 and lesson 2 is linked to opportunity pupils were offered to communicate exclusively in English. Despite many pupils lacked fluency and accuracy, they managed to use little French but much more English to express themselves during interactive activities such as debate, discussion, role-play, and pair work. The lessons helped them immerse into a naturalistic situation of English use. This strength is the result from the application of the language-based approach and the direct method. Both these approach and method gave way to an interactive and extensive oral use of English by the pupils throughout the fulfilment of the class.

The second strength lies in the fact that lesson 2 permitted the integration of the four skills during the teaching process. In fact, applying the language-based approach has helped to involve pupils in activities which enabled them to practise the four skills but in a jointed way. This means that a skill is not improved separately. In this system, the improvement of one skill indirectly entails the improvement of the three other skills. For instance, pupils indirectly improved their listening and speaking skills while involved in a reading activity. Pupils also improved their listening, reading, and even speaking skills while involved in a writing activity such as dictation.

The third strength that was apparent in lesson 1 and lesson 2 was interaction: horizontal[40] and vertical[41] interactions. These interactions were set through the application of student centredness. Horizontal interaction was set through interactive activities such as debate/discussion, role-play, and pair work. However, the vertical interaction resulted from the teacher giving instructions to pupils, or even when he answered their questions to ensure an effective fulfilment of activities.

The fourth strength that was mostly manifest in lesson 2 was pupils' motivation. The motivation resulted from the attractiveness of the didactic materials for the lessons and the interactive activities which implicated all pupils in the teaching-learning process. In fact, the choice of a material dealing with an intriguing and serious theme such as *alcohol intake* made pupils attentive during the class. Such a theme avoided pupils to be bored during class activities. Indeed, involving pupils in a debate or a role-play related to a topic such as *Henchard selling his wife after he has drunk too much alcohol* helped arouse curiosity in pupils. It motivated the latter to interact with their peers and the teacher could deepen their apprehension on the dangerousness of alcohol.

The fifth strength that was evidenced during implementation is mutual education at pupils'. This mutual education resulted from the debate intended to question the *full responsibility of alcohol in Henchard's wife sale*. This activity involved pupils in a debate whereby they expressed opinions and shared ideas in order to agree or not over

---

[40] Horizontal interaction refers to student-student interactions in class activities.
[41] Vertical interaction refers to teacher-student interactions in class activities.

that topic. That activity got each pupil to deepen his/her apprehension of the dangerousness of alcohol from the ideas conveyed by his/her peers over the topic while debating or discussing. Thus, the attractive content and the interactive behaviour of such an activity enabled mutual [horizontal] education among pupils.

VII.3.2. Weaknesses of the Lessons

Unfortunately, we have noticed some weaknesses during the delivery of the lessons: ineffective interactivity in role-play, pupils' lack of vocabulary during debate, time wasted in giving instructions. These weaknesses are presented as follows:

As regards lesson 1, some precious minutes were wasted while giving instructions before activities. It is evident that giving instruction is necessarily opening class activities. Indeed, the teacher should give pupils clear information on the content of each activity before pupils start performing. We noticed that the listening inability caused them to hardly comprehend activity instructions. That situation compelled us to slow down our speaking flow, not only to give activity instructions, but also to repeat sentences for pupils to comprehend the goal of each activity. Because of that situation the fulfilment of activities such as debate, and role-play lasted much longer.

Concerning lesson 2, we involved pupils in a role-play activity to arouse a genuine oral interaction among them. In such an activity as role-play, the script is provided so that the activity has nothing to do with improvisation, to ensure a planned interaction destined to immerse pupils into a real-life situation of English use. However, the fact that pupils discovered the content of the script only at the moment of performance, contributed to creating an adverse effect. Pupils' non-mastery of the script came to be an obstacle to completing of the activity because pupils spent much time reading the script. This situation made the role-play activity look a bit unnatural. Because the performers did not master the script, much time was wasted. Unfortunately, few groups had the opportunity to perform.

During lesson 2, we remarked that the debate was a very challenging activity for some learners. It involved learners in an interactive activity whereby the latter were intended to give arguments fluently and accurately (to defend or oppose a point of view). Unfortunately, some learners conspicuously lacked accuracy while speaking, which caused them to hardly comprehend one another. Evolving in an EFL context, learners are influenced by French and other local dialects. Resultantly, they lack an extensive vocabulary, and make some grammatical mistakes.

These weaknesses noticed during the delivery of these lessons were somehow disappointing aspects during our internship experimentations. They hindered some of our objectives, but as teachers, we are expected to find strategies to circumvent such weaknesses and ensure more effective lesson delivery.

Chapter VIII: Difficulties Encountered and Suggestions

This chapter highlights the hindrances encountered during the fulfilment of this research work. In this chapter, some constructive suggestions are equally provided to circumvent such hindrances.

VIII.1. Difficulties Encountered

Undeniably, our experimentation has suffered from some difficulties during both the inquiry stage and the implementation stage.

VIII.1.1. Inquiry Difficulties

As mentioned previously, our internship happened at Complex Léon MBA. During this internship an inquiry was conducted to collect some data and assess the applicability of our thesis statement. Unfortunately, that inquiry faced some difficulties. First, collecting data from other high schools was impossible because of a full timetable which constrained us to spend most of our time in teaching at Lycée Léon MBA. Second, it was difficult to meet teachers at teachers' headquarters, so it was difficult to interview most of them. Third, the short duration of the internship constrained us to address to questionnaires only to pupils of 4e M_{14} and 2nde S_2 and eight (8) teachers of English we chanced to meet. The original aim was to cover a wider audience, to gather substantial and reliable data for our research, but those encountered handicaps constrained the inquiry to the seventy-nine (79) and eight (8) teachers who were available.

VIII.1.2. Implementation Difficulties

The implementation stage of this research work was difficult due to hindering factors such as a crowded class size, pupils' behaviour about English, and desk arrangement.

One of the classrooms (4^e $M_{14)}$ wherein we implemented the lessons had a large class size. Because of that situation, it was difficult to implicate all pupils in activities such as debate and role-play, which were supposed to make them more active and confident during the learning process. We were constrained to reduce the number of performing pupils to save time. Class size clearly failed our motivational objectives.

The behaviour of some pupils in 2nde S_2 was a difficulty we faced. It hindered our objective to motivate all the 35 pupils in the classroom to make them feel confident to speak English. While most of those pupils were willingly and joyfully implicated in activities, a tiny portion of their peers showed both fear and shyness, when it came to speaking English loudly during the lead-in, the debate, and the role-play.

The desk arrangement is characterised by rows at Lycée Léon MBA. Desks arranged in rows did not facilitate an effective fulfilment of the debate/discussion. Organising a discussion or a debate requires to install pupils in a peculiar setting, suitable for a group debate/discussion. However, installing such a setting was hardly possible because moving these heavy desks would have been time-consuming, and would have contributed to obliterating concentration in pupils. Thus, we were obliged to work in rows to attempt to fulfil our teaching objectives.

VIII.2. Suggestions

In order to facilitate the English language acquisition of Gabonese learners, we would like to address some suggestions to three main entities involved in education activities in Gabon: Institut Pédagogique National (IPN), Ecole Normale Supérieure[42] (ENS), and teachers.

Our first suggestions are politely addressed to **IPN**[43], which is the academic bureau attached to the Ministry of Education. It is in charge of designing and organising the education programmes in Gabon. We suggest that the IPN increase the amount of time allocated to English classes in secondary and high schools. If teachers have some more time, they will be able to cover all their activities and assess pupils' individual performance. It will help them effectively achieve their educational and English teaching objectives.

To **ENS,** we would like to advise it to do its best by appointing teacher trainees for internships earlier than usual. To succeed, the branch in charge of internships at ENS should improve its communication with the board of administrators of high schools and consider their calendar so that teacher trainees could start internship activities the soonest possible. If teacher trainees have a lengthier internship, they will have the opportunity to make thoroughly observations and much time to practise as

---

[42] The Ecole Normale Supérieure (ENS) is State teacher training college in Libreville, since its creation in 1971, it trains high school and secondary school teachers as well as educational advisers and inspectors of primary education.
[43] L'Institut Pédagogique National: The National Pedagogical Institute (NPI) was created in 1984. It is a state institution which is attached to the Ministry of Education in Gabon. This institution is in charge of establishing the school curricula, as well as the selection of the textbooks to be used in classrooms in Gabon. As far as English teaching is concerned, the NPI recommends teachers to both provide pupils with the necessary knowledge linguistic to facilitate their English language acquisition and transmit pupils some educational values for a positive personal development of learners.

well. The application of such an internship policy by ENS will help all teacher trainees to benefit a quite effective training.

We would like to issue some recommendations to teachers of English. We noticed that the dangerousness of alcohol intake is not much echoed to pupils in classes. However, it is a phenomenon which has recurrently jeopardised pupils' lives and studies. For that reason, we recommend teachers to thoroughly explore the alcohol-related contents from *The Mayor of Casterbridge* to sensitise Gabonese learners so far. We advise them to exploit the educational contents in that novel to ensure effective universal value transmission to pupils, to help the latter to have a safe schooling and positive personal development to succeed.

Conclusion of Part Two

In sum, this part presented Lycée Léon MBA, where we experienced a four-month teacher-trainee internship. It is the place where we submitted a questionnaire to seventy-nine (79) pupils in 4e M_{14} and 2nde S_2 and eight (8) teachers to collect data for investigations. We designed and implemented two lesson plans to make the study more practical in that high school.

Despite the weaknesses observed during implementation, there have been some encouraging results (strengths) which helped to confirm that *The Mayor of Casterbridge* by Thomas Hardy could be used for English language acquisition and awareness raising on the dangerousness of alcohol at pupils'. That part also emphasised some difficulties encountered during the training period namely large classes, pupils' shyness and fearful behaviour toward English, desk arrangement in rows, and lack of time. This part was closed by some suggestions to the IPN, ENS, and teachers.

General Conclusion

English language is learned as a foreign language in Gabon's educative system. The question of the acquisition of that language has been debated over in many studies. Seeing that the final goal in language learning is the ability to communicate in the target language with a near-native performance, attaining such a result in an EFL learning context is quite challenging for both teachers and learners. In such a context, teachers of English are impelled to resort to authentic materials to establish naturalistic conditions of English use in the classroom.

This research work was developed in two main parts. Concerning the first part, we firstly clarified the key terms of the topic. Secondly, we proposed some suitable approaches and methods to implement *The Mayor of Casterbridge* in English classes. Thirdly, we highlighted alcohol intake by pupils as being a rampant phenomenon, which threatens the schooling of Gabonese pupils. Fourthly, we proposed some educational articulations related to the topic of alcohol from the book. Lastly, we proposed some teaching activities to implement the novel as an authentic didactic source for English language acquisition and sensitisation to the dangerousness of alcohol. Concerning the second part, we provided a presentation of the place of study. Then, the process of data collection and analysis was given. Next was the successful implementation of two experimental lessons in 4e M_{14} and 2nde S_2 at Lycée Léon National MBA. Some strengths and weaknesses from these lessons were clearly emphasised. Lastly, the obstacles encountered during the study were fully exposed. We closed the study with some suggestions to IPN, ENS, and teachers.

The serious theme of alcohol consumption that derived from the dramatic relation between the protagonist of the novel and alcohol was interesting to pupils. They were eager to debate on the behaviour of Michael Henchard, who sells his wife after drinking much liquor in the storyline. Pupils' opposing viewpoints during such activity have implicitly enabled them to self-educate and educate one another on the harmfulness of alcohol.

The results of the questionnaires' analyses helped legitimise the implementation of the two lessons. All pupils said they would be happy to learn English through *The Mayor of Casterbridge*. The experimental lessons confirmed pupils' opinion about the novel. The result of the implementation lessons was more satisfactory. The activities motivated most of the pupils and aroused their self-confidence to speak despite some slight structural and linguistic inaccuracies.

The research work was also an opportunity to submit some constructive suggestions. Our first suggestions were politely addressed to **IPN**, the academic entity attached to the Ministry of Education, which is in charge of designing and organising education programmes in Gabon. We suggest that the IPN increase the amount of time allocated to English classes in secondary and high schools for teachers to cover all their activities and assess pupils' individual performance. To **ENS,** we highly recommend the institution to do its best to appoint teacher trainees earlier than usual for internships. We think that, if teacher trainees have a lengthier internship, they will have the opportunity to make thorough observations and have much time to practise as well. The application of such an internship management policy by **ENS** will help all teacher trainees to benefit a quite effective training. We would like to offer some recommendations to teachers of English. We have noticed that the dangerousness of alcohol intake is not much echoed to pupils in classes. However, it is a phenomenon which has recurrently jeopardised pupils' lives and studies. For that reason, we recommend teachers to explore the alcohol linked articulations in *The Mayor of Casterbridge* to sensitise Gabonese learners. We advise them to exploit the educational contents in that novel to ensure effective universal value transmission to pupils, so as to help them have a safe schooling and a positive personal development.

REFERENCES

A/ Books

1. Attard, Angele et. al. (2010). *Student Centredness: An insight into Theory and Practice* (1st ed.). Bucharest: European Students' Union.
2. Brinton, D. M., & Master, P. (2001). *New ways in content-based instruction.* Alexandria, VA: TESOL.
3. Cameron, L. (2001). *Teaching Languages to Young Learners* (1st ed.). Cambridge: CUP.
4. Guerin, Wilfred, et al. (2005). *A handbook to critical Approaches to Literature: The Moral-philosophical Approach.* Oxford: Oxford University Press.
5. Hardy, Thomas. (1998). *The Mayor of Casterbridge* (2nd ed.). Oxford: Oxford University Press.
6. Hanes, Melodee. (2012). *Effects and Consequences of Underage Drinking.* Washington, DC: US dept of Justice.
7. Harmer, J. (1991). *The Practice of English Language Teaching.* London: Longman.
8. Richards, J. C., and Rodgers, T. S. (1986). *Approaches and Methods in Language Teaching: A Description and Analysis.* Cambridge: Cambridge University Press.
9. Sanderson, P. (1999). *Using Newspapers in the Classroom.* Cambridge: Cambridge University Press.
10. Saville-Stroike, Muriel. (2006). *Introducing Second Language Acquisition* (1st ed.). Cambridge: Cambridge University Press.
11. Tamo, D. 2009: *The Use of Authentic Materials in Classrooms.* Tirana: University of Tirana.
12. Widdowson, H. (1990): *Aspects of Language Teaching.* Oxford: Oxford University Press.

B/ Journal Articles

1. Anonymous. (2016). *The Biography of Thomas Hardy.* Masterpiece Journal, vol. 4 No. 2. www.masterpiece.org.
2. Dweikat, Khalid, and Shbeitah, Ghada. (2014). An Investigation on Approaches Used by School Teachers in Teaching the Literature Components in EFL Classrooms/English for Palestine Case. *Journal of Al-Quds Open University*, vol. 2 No. 7.

3. Febriani, R., et. al. (2018). Improving the Students' English Language Proficiency: Language-based Aproach. *JALL Journal*, Vol. 2, No. 1.
4. Machemer, P.L. and Crawford, P. (2007). 'Student Perceptions of Active Learning in a Large Cross-Disciplinary Classroom.' *Active Learning in Higher Education*, Vol 8, N°1.
5. Obandja Boyo, Ralph. (2021). Using Brexit-Related Contents to Reinforce Gabonese Learners' English Language Acquisition. *JRSPELT*, Vol. 5, Issue 28, pp. 1–9.
6. _____. (2021). A Christmas Carol by Charles Dickens: An Authentic Didactic Source for English Language Acquisition and Moral Value Teaching. *IJCSRR*. Vol. 4, Issue 11, pp. 1585–1591.
7. Peacock, M. (1997). The Effect of Authentic Materials on the Motivation of EFL Learners. *ELT Journal*, vol. 51, Issue 2, pp. 144-156.
8. Rahman, Fathu. (2016). The Strategy of Teaching Literature Through Language-Based Method: A Communicative Approach. *FIB UNHAS*, vol. 3, No. 4.
9. Savvidou, Christine. (2004). An Integrated Approach to Teaching Literature in the EFL Classroom. *The Internet TESL Journal*, vol. 10, No. 12.
10. Tsui, L. (2002). Fostering Critical Thinking Through Effective Pedagogy: Evidence from Four Institutional Case Studies. *The Journal of Higher Education*, 73:(6): 740-763.
11. Van Eekelen, I.M., Boshuizen, H.P.A and Vermunt, J.D (2005). Self-Regulation in Higher Education Teacher Learning. *Higher Education*, Issue 50, pp. 447-471.

C/ Online News Articles

1. Abogho, N. (2018). Une jeunesse Prise au piège de l'alcool. *Gabonews*. Libreville, Gabon. http://gabonews.com/fr/actus/societe/article/une-jeunesse-prise-au-piege-de-l-alcool. Accessed on 10 June 2022.
2. Admin. (2011). Gabon: Les élèves de 4e sensibilisés aux méfaits des drogues et d'une sexualité précoce. *ExcelAfrica*. Libreville, Gabon. https://www.excelafrica.com/2011/02/03/gabon-les-eleves-de-4e-sensibilises-aux-mefaits-des-drogues-et-dune-sexualite-prec/. Accessed on 10 June 2022.
3. Gabonews. (2011). Deux élèves du Lycée d'État de Ndéndé exclus pour consommation d'Alcool pendant les heures de cours. Libreville, Gabon. https://www.bdpmodwoam.org/articles/2011/10/29/deux-eleves-du-lycee-detat-de-ndende-exclus-pour-consommation-dalcool-pendant-les-heures. Accessed 10 June 2022.

4. LegiGabon. (2019). Les débits de boissons à proximité des établissements scolaires. Libreville, Gabon. Https://www.legigabon.com/single-post/2020/02/16/les-débits-de-boissons-a-proximité-des-établissements-scolaires. Accessed on 12 June 2022.
5. LNNA. (2022). Consommation d'alcool : le Gabon une fois de plus premier du continent. *Ethique Media Gabon.* Libreville, Gabon.
   Consommation d'alcool : le Gabon une fois de plus premier du continent - Éthique Média Gabon (ethiquemediagabon.com) Accessed on 28 September 2022.
6. La rédaction. (2019). Gabon: Quand l'Alcool côtoie la Jeunesse dans les temples du savoir. *Voxpopuli241*.Libreville, Gabon. https://vxp241.com/2019/09/11/gabon-quand-lalcool-cotoie-la-jeunesse-dans-les-temples-du-savoir/. Accessed on 10 June 2022.
7. La rédaction. (2019). Alcool et tabac: Agir pour le Gabon sensibilise les enfants. *L'Union*. Libreville, Gabon. https://www.union.sonapresse.com/gabon-culture-societe/alcool-et-tabac-agir-pour-le-gabon-sensibilise-les-enfants-20723. Accessed on 11 June 2022.
8. La rédaction. (2018). Lutte contre le tabac et l'alcool: Le Gouvernement a capitulé, selon Agir pour le Gabon. *Gabon Matin*. Libreville, Gabon. http://gabonmatin.com/lutte-contre-le-tabac-et-l-alcool-le-gouvernement-a-capitule-selon-agir-pour-le.html. Accessed on 12 June 2022.
9. Mbeng Essone, Lyonnel. (2022). Camélia Ntoutoume-Leclercq va-t-elle fermer les bars à proximité des écoles, collèges et lycées ? *Gabon Media Time*, Libreville, Gabon. https://www.gabonmediatime.com/gabon-camelia-ntoutoume-leclercq-va-t-elle-fermer-les-bars-a-proximite-des-ecoles-colleges-et-lycees/. Accessed on 5 August 2022.
10. Musavu, Alix-Ida. (2019). Bars à proximité d'écoles: bientôt la fermeture par la police. *GabonReview*. Libreville, Gabon. https://www.gabonreview.com/bars-a-proximite-decoles-bientot-la-fermeture-par-la-police/. Accessed on 18 June 2022.

D/ Miscellaneous

1. Anonymous. (2020). Les sept rôles de l'enseignant en classe. *BienEnseigner Blog*. Paris, France. <https://www.bienenseigner.com/les-7-role-de-lenseignant-en-classe/>. Accessed on 12 June 2022.
2. Journal Officiel de la République gabonaise. (1970). Décret n° 00864/PR/MI/MD/CI du 30 juillet 1970 portant sur la règlementation des débits

de boissons en République gabonaise. Libreville, Gabon. http://journal-officiel.ga . Accessed on 14 June 2022.
3. _____. (1976). Ordonance n° 59/76 du 1er octobre 1976 portant sur la protection des mineurs. Journal Officiel N°24 Du 25 Octobre 1976. Libreville, Gabon. http://journal-officiel.ga/14511-59-76/. Accessed on 14 June 2022.
4. _____. (2012). Décret n° 0408/PR/MISPID du 26 septembre 2012 fixant les conditions d'ouverture et d'exploitation des débits de boissons en République gabonaise. Journal Officiel N°130 Du 7 Septembre 2012. Libreville, Gabon. http://journal-officiel.ga/2404-0408-pr-mispid/. Accessed on 14 June 2022.
5. Weston, Pauline. (2022). From the Regency Era to the Victorian Era. *Fashion-Era*. London, United Kingdom. https://fashion-era.com/victorians.htm. Accessed on 15 June 2022.
6. Yannsteph. (2011). Les droits et devoirs de l'éducateur. *Overblog*. Yaoundé, Cameroun. http://meliyann-info-tic.over-blog.com/article-chapitre-vi-les-droits-et-les-devoirs-de-l-educateur-64617713.html. Accessed on 12 June 2022.

E/ Master's Theses

1. EYANG, Mareille. (2020). *Teaching English through Some African Literary Texts to Improve Pupils' Language Acquisition: The Case of the Second Cycle.* Mémoire de MASTER. Libreville: École Normale Supérieure.

F/ Audio-Visual Sources

Audio Book

- Audiobooks Unleashed. (2020). *The Mayor of Casterbridge by Thomas Hardy*. YouTube. https://www.youtube.com/watch?v=e_Fq2y6c3s8. Accessed on 15 June 2022.

Movie

- Thacker, David. (2003). *The Mayor of Casterbridge*. LWT and Sally Head Productions.

TV Series

- Giles, David. (1978). *The Mayor of Casterbridge*. BBC2.

G/ Dictionaries

- *Collins Cobuild English Language Dictionary* (1992)
- *Longman Online Dictionary of Language Teaching and Applied Linguistics* (2011)

APPENDICES

Appendix 1. Pupils' Questionnaire.

Question 1: vous apprenez l'anglais depuis…?

- o 3 ans
- o 4 ans
- o 5 ans
- o 6 ans
- o 7 ans

Question 2: Quel est votre niveau en anglais ?

- o Aucun maniement des quatre facultés
- o Niveau intermédiaire
- o Maniement avancé

Question 3: Avez-vous déjà fait des jeux de rôle pendant le cours d'anglais ?

- o Oui
- o Non

Question 4: Avez-vous déjà fait des débats pendant le cours d'anglais?

- o Oui
- o Non

Question 5: Quels sont les thèmes les plus évoqués par le professeur d'anglais ?

- o Les grosses précoces et les MSTs
- o La délinquance juvénile
- o Les drogues

Question 6: Quels sont les supports didactiques les plus utilisés par le professeur d'anglais ?

- o Le texte
- o Les vidéos
- o Les audios

Question 7: Aimez-vous les histoires qui se terminent par une leçon de morale ? Justifiez.

Question 8: Avez-vous déjà bu de l'alcool ?

   o Oui
   o Non

Question 9: Est-ce que boire de l'alcool est une bonne chose ?

   o Oui
   o Non

Question 10: Seriez-vous content d'apprendre l'anglais à travers The Mayor Of Casterbridge ?

   o Oui
   o Nom

Appendix 2. Teachers' Questionnaire

1. What is your qualification?
2. How long have you been teaching English?
3. Do you design clear objectives when you prepare your lesson?
4. What subjects do you often teach to pupils? a) Economics b) Politics c) d) entertainment e) Other.
5. What type of supports do you often use? a) Texts b) Videos c) Audios d) Other.
6. What is the impact of your activities on pupils?
7. Have you ever used a literary content as a didactic support?
8. From which literature are these literary contents taken? a) African literature b) American literature c) British literature.
9. Have you ever read *The Mayor of Casterbridge by Thomas Hardy?*
10. Have you ever used *TMC* as a didactic support?
11. Using *TMC* to teach English to learners would be: a) Interesting b) Boring c) Risky? Justify.

Appendix 3. Text: Michael Henchard Becomes a Teetotaler[1].

Shortly after selling his wife and baby daughter because he was drunk, Michael Heanchard entered the church to take his oath. The hay-trusser deposited his basket by the font and walked up the nave till he reached the altar. He opened the gate to enter the sacrarium, where he seemed to feel a sense of the strangeness for a moment. Then, he knelt upon the foot-pace. Dropping his head upon the closed book which lay on the Communion table, he said aloud: I, Michael Henchard, on this morning of the sixteenth of September, do take an oath before God here in this solemn place that I will avoid all strong liquors for twenty-one years to come. And I swear this upon the Book before me. Therefore, if I break this oath, may I become a blind and miserable man forever. When he had said it and kissed the big book, Henchard arose, and felt happy to start a life in a new direction.

1. A person who abstains from drinking alcohol.

Adapted from *The Mayor of Casterbridge* by Thomas Hardy, pp. 19–20.

Appendix 4. Text/Script: Drunk, Henchard sells his Wife Susan for five guineas.

After eating his porridge mixed with some liquor, Michael Henchard chain drinks four basins of liquor. Suddenly, he goes drunk and starts to talk nastily to his wife [Susan] as well. He accuses her of being the source of his miserable financial condition. Shortly after, Michael decides to sell Susan with their baby daughter [Elisabeth-Jane] to a sailor [Mr Newson] in an auction for a five-guinea amount of money.

Henchard: I married at eighteen, like the fool that I was; and this is the consequence of it. I haven't more than fifteen shillings in the world, and yet I am a good experienced hand in my line.

Henchard: For my part I don't see why men who have got wives, and don't want 'em, shouldn't get rid of 'em. Hey? Why, begad, I'd sell my wife this minute, if anybody would buy her!

Henchard: Well, then, now is your chance; I am open to an offer for this gem of creation.

Susan: Michael, you have talked this nonsense in public places before. A joke is a joke, but you may make it once too often, mind!

Henchard: I know I've said it before; I meant it. -All I want is a buyer. Will someone among you buy my goods?

Susan: Mike, Mike, this is getting serious. Oh—too serious!

Henchard: Will anybody buy her? Her present owner is not at all to her liking!

Henchard: Now, who's auctioneer?

Auctioneer: I am! Who'll make an offer for this lady? She's worth two guineas!

Saleswoman: Behave yourself moral, good man, for Heaven's love! Ah, what a cruelty is the poor soul married to!

Henchard: Set the price higher, auctioneer!

Auctioneer: Now, the lady is worth three guineas … four guineas.

Henchard: I'll sell her for five guineas to any man that will pay me the money and treat her well; and he shall have her for ever, and never hear aught of me.

Henchard: Do any body give it? - Yes or no?

Mr Newson: Yes, I do!

Henchard: Saying is one thing, and paying is another. Where's the money?

Susan: Before you go further Michael, listen to me. If you touch that money, I and this girl go with the man. Mind, it is a joke no longer.

Henchard: I take the money: the sailor takes you. That's plain enough. It has been done elsewhere and why not here!

Susan: Mike, I've lived with you a couple of years, and had nothing but temper. Now I'm no more to you; I'll try my luck elsewhere. It will be better for me and Elizabeth-Jane both. So good-bye.

Adapted from *The Mayor of Casterbridge* by Thomas Hardy, p.5-20.

Appendix 5

Dictation: The Physical Portrait of Micheal Henchard.

Micheal Henchard was of fine figure, swarthy, and stern in aspect; and he showed in profile a facial angle so slightly inclined as to be almost perpendicular. He wore a short jacket of brown corduroy, newer than the remainder of his suit, which was a fustian waistcoat with white horn buttons, breeches of the same, tanned leggings, and a straw hat overlaid with black glazed canvas. At his back he carried by a looped strap a rush basket from which protruded at one end the crutch of a hay knife, a wimble for hay-bonds being also visible in the aperture. His measured springless walk was the walk of the skilled countryman as distinct from the desultory shamble of the general labourer.

Adapted from *The Mayor of Casterbridge* by Thomas Hardy, p. 5.

Appendix 6

Source: Google Chrome images accessed on July 10, 2022

We have made every effort to acknowledge all sources, but if we have inadvertently overlooked any, we shall be pleased to make the necessary arrangements at the first opportunity.